RANCHO CUCAMONGA
PUBLIC LIBRARY

D1218828

COMPREHENSIVE RESEARCH
AND STUDY GUIDE

Christina
Rossetti

EDITED AND WITH AN INTRODUCTION
BY HAROLD BLOOM

CURRENTLY AVAILABLE

COMPREHENSIVE RESEARCH
AND STUDY GUIDE

Christina Rossetti

CHELSEA HOUSE
PUBLISHERS
A Haights Cross Communications Company

Philadelphia

RANCHO CUCAMONGA
PUBLIC LIBRARY

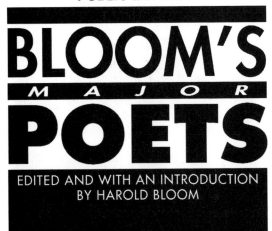

BLOOM'S
MAJOR
POETS

EDITED AND WITH AN INTRODUCTION
BY HAROLD BLOOM

© 2004 by Chelsea House Publishers, a subsidiary of
Haights Cross Communications.

A Haights Cross Communications ✦ Company

http://www.chelseahouse.com

Introduction © 2005 by Harold Bloom.

All rights reserved. No part of this publication may be reproduced or
transmitted in any form or by any means without the written permission
of the publisher.

Printed and bound in the United States of America.

First Printing
1 3 5 7 9 8 6 4 2

Library of Congress Cataloging-in-Publication Data

Christina Rossetti / Harold Bloom, editor.
    p. cm. — (Bloom's major poets)
  Includes bibliographical references and index.
  ISBN 0-7910-7892-2
  1. Rossetti, Christina Georgina, 1830-1894—Criticism and interpretation.
  2. Women and literature—England—History—19th century.
I. Bloom, Harold. II. Series.
  PR5238.C49 2004
  821'.8—dc22
                                        2004013703

Contributing Editor: Samuel Arkin

Cover design by Keith Trego

Layout by EJB Publishing Services

All links and web addresses were checked and verified to be correct at the time
of publication. Because of the dynamic nature of the web, some addresses and
links may have changed since publication and may no longer be valid.

Every effort has been made to trace the owners of copyrighted material and
secure copyright permission. Articles appearing in this volume generally
appear much as they did in their original publication with little to no editorial
changes. Those interested in locating the original source will find bibliograph-
ic information on the first page of each article as well as in the bibliography
and acknowledgments sections of this volume.

CONTENTS

USER'S GUIDE

This volume is designed to present biographical, critical, and bibliographical information on the author and the author's best-known or most important poems. Following Harold Bloom's editor's note and introduction is a concise biography of the author that discusses major life events and important literary accomplishments. A critical analysis of each poem follows, tracing significant themes, patterns, and motifs in the work. As with any study guide, it is recommended that the reader read the poem beforehand and have a copy of the poem being discussed available for quick reference.

A selection of critical extracts, derived from previously published material, follows each thematic analysis. In most cases, these extracts represent the best analysis available from a number of leading critics. Because these extracts are derived from previously published material, they will include the original notations and references when available. Each extract is cited, and readers are encouraged to check the original publication as they continue their research. A bibliography of the author's writings, a list of additional books and articles on the author and their work, and an index of themes and ideas conclude the volume.

ABOUT THE EDITOR

Harold Bloom is Sterling Professor of the Humanities at Yale University. He is the author of over 20 books, and the editor of more than 30 anthologies of literary criticism.

Professor Bloom's works include *Shelley's Mythmaking* (1959), *The Visionary Company* (1961), *Blake's Apocalypse* (1963), *Yeats* (1970), *A Map of Misreading* (1975), *Kabbalah and Criticism* (1975), *Agon: Toward a Theory of Revisionism* (1982), *The American Religion* (1992), *The Western Canon* (1994), and *Omens of Millennium: The Gnosis of Angels, Dreams, and Resurrection* (1996). *The Anxiety of Influence* (1973) sets forth Professor Bloom's provocative theory of the literary relationships between the great writers and their predecessors. His most recent books include *Shakespeare: The Invention of the Human*, a 1998 National Book Award finalist, *How to Read and Why* (2000), *Stories and Poems for Extremely Intelligent Children of All Ages* (2001), *Genius: A Mosaic of One Hundred Exemplary Creative Minds* (2002), and *Hamlet: Poem Unlimited* (2003).

Professor Bloom earned his Ph.D. from Yale University in 1955 and has served on the Yale faculty since then. He is a 1985 MacArthur Foundation Award recipient and served as the Charles Eliot Norton Professor of Poetry at Harvard University in 1987–88. In 1999 he was awarded the prestigious American Academy of Arts and Letters Gold Medal for Criticism. Professor Bloom is the editor of several other Chelsea House series in literary criticism, including BLOOM'S MAJOR SHORT STORY WRITERS, BLOOM'S MAJOR NOVELISTS, BLOOM'S MAJOR DRAMATISTS, BLOOM'S MODERN CRITICAL INTERPRETATIONS, BLOOM'S MODERN CRITICAL VIEWS, BLOOM'S BIOCRITIQUES, BLOOM'S GUIDES, BLOOM'S MAJOR LITERARY CHARACTERS, and BLOOM'S PERIOD STUDIES.

EDITOR'S NOTE

My Introduction centers upon *Goblin Market* as an allegory of Christina Rossetti's struggle for poetic individuation against the powerful influence of John Keats.

Nine analyses of *Goblin Market* follow, all of them useful, but those by Herbert Tucker and Jerome McGann seem to me truly distinguished instances of authentic scholarly interpretation.

On the poignant "Remember," I emphasize the five different meanings the title receives in the sonnet, while Margaret Reynolds reminds us how riddling this astonishing lyric poet tended to be, since doubling is her characteristic mode.

"A Birthday" is seen by Lynda Palazzo as set in the Rossetti family's context, after which the superb "Up-Hill" is illuminated in very contrasting ways by Jerome McGann's theological learning and John Hollander's poetics of rhetoric.

INTRODUCTION

Harold Bloom

Christina Rossetti (1830–94) is one of a handful of major English devotional poets, together with John Donne, George Herbert, Richard Crashaw, Henry Vaughn, and her contemporary, the Jesuit Gerard Manley Hopkins. One might expect the beloved sister of Dante Gabriel Rossetti to manifest a marked difference from other poets of religious sensibility. Like the Pre-Raphaelites, her style and procedures stem from Keats and Tennyson, rather than Donne and Herbert, but then Hopkins also is Keatsian in mode.

Goblin Market doubtless is Christina Rossetti's masterpiece, and rightly has become a favorite text for feminist literary criticism. It fascinates and disturbs me, and though I have included it complete in two anthologies, I never have commented upon the poem, for reasons I can only surmise. In a sense it is poetry for children, though indeed they have to be extremely intelligent children of all ages. Thus they could resist the current academic interpretations: Marxist, feminist, lesbian-incestous, or imagistic self-gratification, at once erotic, mercantile, and even vampiric.

There certainly is a struggle going on in *Goblin Market*, but it seems to me an agon for poetic incarnation, for the establishment of a strong poetic self. I don't suppose that Christina Rossetti would have accepted John Keats's Scene of Instruction less ambivalently if he had been a woman, since strong poets are not particularly given to communal quilt-making. What troubles *Goblin Market* is not only Keats's magnificent oxymoronic rhetoric but also his naturalistic humanism. Keatsian eroticism is totally free of the melancholy sound of church bells. Christina Rossetti's intense faith was intricately fused with an erotic temperament as exuberant as her brother Dante Gabriel Rossetti's, and her lifelong renunciation (so far as we know) of sexual experience testifies to a rather frightening strength of will, or of faith if you would have it so. The Tempter in *Goblin Market* is in any case John Keats and not John Keble, or Romanticism rather than the Oxford Movement of Anglican Revivalism.

I hasten to insist that I find it grotesque to identify the Goblins as male precursor poets: Milton, Keats, Tennyson, and D.G. Rossetti and his friends. The nursery rhyme stylistics of *Goblin Market* are wonderfully effective swerves away from Keatsian celebrations of natural abundance, but they defend against glories of language, and not against gendered dangers.

That *Goblin Market* is an open-ended allegory is its finest attribute. Such irony invests deeply in the fantastic, challenging us to behold our own idiosyncratic phantasmagoras. Perhaps Friedrich Schlegel's definition of irony as the "permanent parabasis of meaning" could not be better exemplified than by Christina Rossetti's most ambitious poem.

BIOGRAPHY OF

Christina Rossetti

Christina Georgina Rossetti was born in London on December 5, 1830, to Gabriele and Frances (Polidori) Rossetti. Both of her parents were of strong religious temperament. Her father was an Italian living in exile, and her mother was of Italian and English origin. The house she was born into was quite lively, playing host to visiting Italian revolutionaries and writers, but she was also subject to the teaching and religious devotion of her mother Frances. Her father Gabriele was a poet and translator, and her uncle John Palidori was Byron's physician and author of "The Vampyre."

Rossetti's home was bilingual, and all of the children in her family were artistic and scholarly. The oldest, Maria Francesca, was a Dante scholar, and her brother Gabriel Charles Dante (who would change his name to Dante Gabriel) became a poet and a painter. William Michael, the younger of the two brothers, became a critic and biographer, and later edited and published commentaries on the poems and letters of his siblings.

Christina is said to have been a very spirited child, and there are wild reports about her youthful temper. These anecdotes stand in contrast to the descriptions of the poet by her brother William in the biography he wrote, which gives us an image of a restrained, almost docile poet with self-discipline to spare. Her early childhood was punctuated by visits to her maternal grandfather's country home, which was surrounded by fruit trees and fields. Eventually, this same grandfather would move to the city and set up a printing press, which would then print Rossetti's first volume of poetry, "Verses: Dedicated to Her Mother". In 1848 she became engaged to James Collinson, one of the minor Pre-Raphaelites. His reversion to Roman Catholicism would soon end the engagement.

In 1853 Christina's father became ill, and his eyesight began to deteriorate. Christina and her mother started a day school to try and support the family, which was not sustainable. After this episode Christina would become more and more reclusive, suffering from a recurring illness which was sometimes diagnosed as angina and sometimes tuberculosis. Her own family feared for her health starting at a young age, starting as early as 1845, and she seems to have been in a near constant state of nervous exhaustion.

The Rossetti children worshiped their mother, but Christina's relationship was especially close with her. Due in part to her bad health, her mother served as both confidant and nurse, and all of Christina's books of poetry were dedicated to her. Both women shared a clear and strong sense of spiritual devotion. Rossetti herself was influenced by the Oxford Movement, which wanted to restore a sense of Catholic Grandeur to the Anglican church, reinforcing the ritualistic elements of the Catholic service. Later in her life, Christina would write extensive commentaries on parts of the bible, and she was a strict observer of fast days and the liturgical calendar.

It is important, however, not to dwell on what is outwardly pious in the biography of Rossetti. She remained friends with her brothers her entire life. William was a free-thinking atheist, and Dante Gabriel is legendary for his sensuality. In addition, her letters show the extent of her contact with other poets and her generosity with young writers. She was also a member of a group called the 'Pre-Raphaelite Brotherhood,' formed in 1848 by her brothers. She was not allowed to attend their late night meetings, but her early poems were published by the brotherhood's journal, "The Germ."

Her first publicly printed book of poetry was "Goblin Market and Other Poems," published in 1862 to widespread acclaim and popularity. In 1866, Rossetti was again proposed to, this time by Charles Bagot Cayley, a Dante scholar and former student of her father. William, after her death, found a series of love poems in Christina's desk that suggest that she loved Cayley very deeply, although while living, she refused him because of his religious skepticism.

She continued to write and in the 1870s to work for the Society for Promoting Christian Knowledge. She was troubled physically by neuralgia and emotionally by Dante's breakdown in 1872. The last 12 years of her life, after his death in 1882, were outwardly quiet ones. She died of cancer December 29, 1894.

CRITICAL ANALYSIS OF
"Goblin Market"

Goblin Market is a poem full of lists that describes something to be avoided, but the poet seems to take pleasure in this act of prohibited description. Each fruit seems more luscious and delightful than the last, and generally the atmosphere of the poem is one where objects are barely allowed to remain inert. For people, one epithet is not enough, and even those must be listed:

> Laura stretched her gleaming neck
> Like a rush-imbedded swan,
> Like a lily from the beck,
> Like a moonlit poplar branch,
> Like a vessel at the launch
> When its last restraint is gone.

Restraint is a condition felt according to the remembrance of its future parting. The description is of Laura listening to the goblin men, and one is not sure whether the dock is restraining the vessel, or even if the vessel wants to leave. The very mechanism of simile has been somewhat impugned by the goblin men, whose voices sound "like voice of doves", "kind and full of loves / in the pleasant weather". In the poem, two sisters who live together, Laura and Lizie, are exposed to a group of goblin merchants as they go about the nightly task of gathering water from a local brook. While we are told that the goblins are active "morning and evening", it is at "twilight" that their voices seem most audible, when "sound" is most "to eye". It is Laura who succumbs, who "chooses" to linger, and she is lulled by the voices of the goblin men, voices that sound to her "like voice of doves / cooing all together". And it is this relation that is troubling throughout the poem. What is initially conceived as a malign phantasmal presence—that of the goblins—is also part of the beneficent aspect of fantasy. There is a thin line between the persuasive, goblin-like exhortations of the vendors and the cooing of doves that "sounded kind and full of loves / in the pleasant weather" which their cries sometimes resemble. The voice of the goblin is at once "shrill" and iterable and capable of achieving "tones as smooth as honey". The gloss that this complexity deserves may not be the simple one, among others, that the poem affords: "Twilight is not good for maidens".

There is, in the poem, a synthetic principle that extends from the perils of the natural world to the bastion of the human. It is a liquid one. I take an example from just after Laura enters into bargaining with the Goblins:

"Buy from us with golden curl."
She clipped a precious golden lock,
She dropped a tear more rare than pearl,
Then sucked their fruit globes fair or red:
Sweeter than honey from the rock,
Stronger than man rejoicing wine,
Clearer than water flowed the juice.

The standard of comparison, of value, is as follows. The lock of hair is as valuable as the actual money that Laura is unable to produce. The tear that Laura lets fall, of joy and of sorrow both, is "more rare than pearl", and so in some sense beyond nature, while related to it by comparison. The liquid juice of the goblin fruit, which is omnipresent during the story, is "clearer than water". After tasting it, Laura "knew not was it night or day", and is clearly in the twilight. However, it is the principle of luscious simile-based description itself that may be as sweet as the imagined fruit; regardless, the poem forces us to conceive of a material pleasure (with the imagination of the body) in order to register the weight of the figurative.

The punishment for such pleasure, we learn from the example of Jeanie, is to stay "ever in the noonlight". This inspires a state of longing in which the symptoms are a watering mouth and a "longing for the night" that feels like an "absent dream". This resembles, curiously, the need that brings the women to the brook each night, and so makes them vulnerable, that of thirst. It is in the evening that the sisters go "with pitchers to the reedy brook", and it is the imagery of water in the poem that makes its appeal general. The image of longing for things past in the poem involves tears:

> One day remembering her kernal-stone
> She set it by a wall that faced the south;
> Dewed it with tears, hoped for a root,
> Watched for a waxing shoot,
> But there came none;
> It never saw the sun,
> It never felt the trickling moisture run:
> While with sunk eyes and faded mouth
> She dreamed of melons, as a traveller sees
> False waves in desert drouth
> With shake of leaf-crowned trees,
> And burns the thirstier in the sandful breeze.

It is worth remembering that the source of the goblin fruits sweetness is involved in what they drink. Laura imagines that it is thanks to the "pure wave that they drink", a brook into which lilies drop their "sugar sweet sap", that the fruit is so good. Longing is an image of thirst just as thirst is a cause of longing. Laura is able to taste the fruit once, and suffers passively afterwards, by denial. The night that Laura goes to repeat her feast, only her uninitiated sister can hear the goblins, and Laura goes home "her pitcher dripping all the way", a victim of "baulked desire".

Human want is the cause of the market in this poem, and money functions both when actual money is only gestured towards, and when real silver coins are being used. Symbols are exchangeable in the poem, as a lock of hair can seem to replace a coin. It is, however, also with a coin that Lizzie rescues her sister. She hands the goblins a silver piece that is then returned to her, which makes possible, in a figurative way, the return of her sisters hair, who can only regain her youth once Lizzie has attempted to buy fruit for her. It is the sound of the returned coin bouncing in Lizzie's purse that restores the fictive music. She hears the coin "bouncing in her purse / its bounce was music to her ear. / She ran and ran / as if she feared some goblin man". Like Laura, Lizzie after her exchange with the Goblins "knew not was it night or day", but her confusion is an "inward laughter" rather than melancholy.

The exchanges between the sisters and the goblin men are resolved when one of the sisters, Lizzie, decides to exchange herself for Laura. Laura gives us a version of this: "Lizzie, Lizzie, have you tasted / for my sake the fruit forbidden?" It is only after this moment that Laura's eyes can be, somewhat paradoxically, "refreshed" by "tears", tears that drop "like rain / after long sultry drouth". It is also after Laura exchanges her own fate for that of Lizzie that we are given the ultimate description of Laura's condition, a description made possible by her re-tasting the fruit from off of her sister's body, and finding it bitter and strange:

> Pleasure past and anguish past,
> Is it death or is it life?
>
> Life out of death.
> That night long Lizzie watched by her,
> Counted her pulse's flagging stir,
> Felt for her breath,
> Held water to her lips, and cooled her face
> With tears

CRITICAL VIEWS ON
"Goblin Market"

STEVEN CONNOR ON THE LINKS BETWEEN "GOBLIN MARKET" AND ROSSETTI'S OTHER WORKS

[Steven Connor is Professor of Modern Literature and Theory at Birkbeck College, University of London. He has also written and edited books on James Joyce, Charles Dickens, and Samuel Beckett. His recent publications include *The Book of Skin*, and *Dumbstruck: A History of Ventriloquism*.]

Goblin Market remains one of the most persistently puzzling poems of the nineteenth century; familiarity has seemed to increase rather than to diminish our uncertainty about its form, style, meaning, and even content. The poem has been treated too much, however, as sui generis, without reference to the rest of Christina Rossetti's work and especially to her other writing for children.[1] The aim of this brief essay is to make the links between her other work and *Goblin Market* a little clearer and thus to throw light on some of the peculiarities of this poem, as well as to suggest ways in which Christina Rossetti's poetry as a whole shares with *Goblin Market* the capacity to unsettle.

First, it is important to note the power which nursery rhyme had over Christina Rossetti; indeed the title of the volume of nursery rhymes which she published hints at the kinds of attraction which the form had for her, particularly its tendency to organize meaning and expression in terms of pair and antithesis. Critics have noted this predominance of pairings and opposites in Christina Rossetti's own poetry: the pairing relationship of sisterhood, for instance,[2] or the pairing and counterposing of different conditions of existence, the earthly and the transcendental, or indeed the dualistic sense displayed in many of the very titles of the poems, such as "Life and Death," "He and She," "One Foot in Sea and One on Shore," and "From Sunset to Star-Rise."[3] This pattern is restated in the dialogic form of many of her lyrics and similarly in many of the nursery rhymes in *Sing-Song* which are poised in the hesitant space between question and answer:

Why did baby die,
Making Father sigh,
Mother cry?

Flowers that bloom to die
Make no reply
Of "Why?"
But bow and die.[4]

But more than this, Christina Rossetti found in nursery rhyme that same attention to the density of language which is a feature of many of her lyrics. Released from reference to the real world, or even to a strongly experienced world of feeling, her verse often enacts in the shifting of its appositions a drama which is to be apprehended at the level of the signifier:

Ah changed and cold, how changed and very cold,
    With stiffened smiling lips and cold calm eyes!
        Changed, yet the same. ("Dead Before Death," pp. 313–314)

There's blood between us, love, my love,
There's father's blood, there's brother's blood;
And blood's a bar I cannot pass. ("The Convent Threshold," p. 340)

This shifting is displayed in the poem "Cobwebs," where the actual subject of the poem recedes into invisibility under the pressure of the continuous negatives: "no moons or seasons wax or wane, / ... / No bud time, no leaf-falling, there for aye" (p. 317). The subject slips away behind the elaborate dance of denials. One of the attractions of nursery rhyme shown in *Sing-Song* is the opportunity to indulge the expressivity of a language emptied of content. This point is obviously of great importance for the understanding of a poem such as *Goblin Market*, where the apparent garrulousness of the verse is an enactment quite as much as a representation of sexual/linguistic energy. This is not to imply, however, that this kind of poetic language is sprawling or incoherent; we know that Christina Rossetti devoted considerable time to the writing of these nursery rhymes (and their translation into Italian). What follows, in fact, is the conception of language as a game—an essentially closed, self-sustaining activity. Included under the heading of "Poems for Children, and Minor Verse" in William Rossetti's edition of his sister's poetry is a series of poems which testify to Christina Rossetti's interest in language games. There are riddles ("Two Enigmas," "Two Charades," p. 422), alphabets, counting rhymes, sonnets written to bouts-rimés, and playful conceits:

A pin has a head, but has no hair;
A clock has a face, but no mouth there;
Needles have eyes, but they cannot see;
A fly has a trunk without lock or key. (p. 432)

or mnemonics:

O Lady Moon, your horns point toward the east;
    Shine, be increased:
O Lady Moon, your horns point toward the west;
    Wane, be at rest. (p. 442)

The important point about a mnemonic is that it locates within language, within its chimings and assonances, the ordering of experience. The signifier becomes self-motivating, turning the fortuitous into the systematic.

NOTES

1. Aside from the difficult case of *Goblin Market*, Christina Rossetti wrote three works specifically for children: *Sing-Song: A Nursery-Rhyme Book* (London, 1872), *Speaking Likenesses* (London. 1874), and *Maude: A Story for Girls* (London, 1897).

2. See Winston Weathers, "Christina Rossetti: The Sisterhood of Self," *VP*, 3 (1965), 81–89.

3. See, for instance, Theo Dombrowski, "Dualism in the Poetry of Christina Rossetti," *VP*, 14 (1976), 70–76: Friedrich Dubslaff, *Die Sprachform der Lyrik Christina Rossettis* (Halle, 1933), p. 75 ff.

4. *The Poetical Works of Christina Georgina Rossetti*, ed. W.M. Rossetti

(London, 1904), pp. 425–429. Subsequent references to Rossetti's poetry will be cited by page number to this text.

—Steven Connor. "Speaking Likenesses": Language and Repetition in Christina Rossetti's *Goblin Market*. *Victorian Poetry* vol. 22, no. 4, winter 1984: 439–441.

HERBERT F. TUCKER ON "MARKETING" VICTORIAN SOCIETY

[Herbert F. Tucker is Professor of English at the University of Virginia. He specializes in Nineteenth-Century English Literature, and he has written books on Tennyson and Browning. He is also editor of *Victorian Literature 1830–1900* and *A Companion to Victorian Literature and Culture*.]

When Christina Rossetti let it fall that in "Goblin Market" she had written no parable soliciting deep exegesis but a poem to be taken just as it came, she may have meant to wave the hermeneutic white flag. In effect, she was dropping the scented handkerchief. The eldritch embroidery of "Goblin Market" has probably attracted more, and more various, commentary during the last two decades than any other poem of its time. It proves on recent examination to be a poem about communal sorority and also about patriarchal dominion; about the Christian Eucharist and also free self-actualization; about diffusive jouissance and also the therapeutic consolation of a split soul; about anorexia nervosa, vampirism, the adulteration of foodstuffs, absinthe addiction, and the pros and cons of masturbation.[1]
While so many critical allegories can hardly be mutually compatible, taken en masse they fortify every reader's conviction that, whatever "Goblin Market" means, it is a work instinct with sex, drugs, rock and roll, or their Victorian equivalents. Determining what these equivalents might be is a nice task for critical brokerage; lately the smart money has been placed on economics. The readings of the poem that make the most comprehensive sense of its multiplex appeal are the ones that put the *market* back in "Goblin Market," and vice versa; that ask how

Rossetti's masterpiece both, critically reflects upon, and knowingly takes part in, systems of commodity exchange that during her lifetime transformed Victorian society and the terms of her calling as a writer within it.[2] To a series of strong mercantile interpretations published by American scholars during the 1990s I propose adding what marketing practices of the later nineteenth century most conspicuously added to the victorious technologies of capitalism, the element of advertising. The seductions in—and of—"Goblin Market" were early warnings—and exploitations—of Victorian styles of market penetration that, inasmuch as they ventured to influence behavior by reorienting desire through language, had every claim on the attention of contemporary poets. This was especially true for a poet of Christina Rossetti's age: born in 1830, and cresting the prime of life in 1862 when her *Goblin Market* volume was published, she was young enough to feel the new pitch of Victorian advertisement as keyed particularly to her generation's susceptibilities; yet she was old enough to know better, having grown up under a more naive promotional dispensation.

From this historically privileged vantage the whole story of "Goblin Market" in a sense flows, and it goes like this: Laura and Lizzie, two look-alike alliterative sisters, live together alone keeping cows, chickens, and bees in a rural neighborhood that happens to be frequented by goblin men peddling domestic and imported fruit in the open air around breakfast and supper time. The sisters are of indeterminate age: young maidens, clearly; yet old enough to be independent of any parental supervision or truant officer, to know a cautionary tale or two about those goblin costermongers, and to qualify for illustration as stunners— initially by the poet's brother Dante Gabriel in the first edition of 1862 and then a century later in an unbowdlerized, cut-to-the-chase version in *Playboy* magazine that, in case it has not come to your attention on some former occasion, has been generously represented in a recent article by Lorraine Kooistra.[3] One evening Laura succumbs to the goblins' mouth-watering sales pitch and, though penniless, contracts to barter a lock of her hair for all the fruit she can eat. Coming home in a nigh bulimic buzz, she brushes aside her sister Lizzie's scolding with a promise to go out again the next night and get more fruit for both of them. As that next night falls, Laura finishes up her farm chores and goes out cruising for goblin. But she can't score: frustrated at first to find no goblin on the scene, she then learns to her horror that, while Lizzie can hear the vendors as usual, she herself has gone stone-deaf to their cry.

Sick with desire, Laura wastes away to the point where Lizzie overcomes scruple and decides to act as her sister's proxy, taking a penny in her purse and letting the goblins know she's ready to deal. But—in a scene to which we shall return—when Lizzie orders a pennysworth of fruit on a takeout basis, the goblins insist that she feast on the spot like her sister. Lizzie declines and demands her money back, at which point the goblin team really gets down to business. They mount a hard sell that escalates from courtesy and advice to insult and threat, cresting at length in the apotheosis of sales force: resorting to outright personal violence, they become pushers indeed, crushing fruit against her mouth— which will not open, however, either to protest or to taste—and drizzling juice down her chin and neck. Finally the goblins take no for an answer, reject the penny, and vanish underground or into thin air. Lizzie races home in an afterglow of ecstatic renunciation (remember, it's a Victorian poem) and invites Laura to "Hug me, kiss me, suck my juices ... Eat me, drink me, love me" (don't worry, it's a Victorian poem).[4] Aghast at Lizzie's apparent sacrifice, yet obedient to an addict's need, Laura ingests the pulpy juice, only to have it work as a homeopathic antidote kicking her into a high-speed delirium, from which she recovers Completely Cured. An epilogue fast-forwards to later years: both sisters now being married, Laura makes a habit of summoning her daughters and nieces—nephews, sons, and husbands somehow need not apply—to hear her tale of trespass, waste, and redemption and to learn its lesson that "there is no friend like a sister" (562).

II

Few readers have been entirely at ease with this overdetermined final scene of instruction. But a convenient back door opens into the poem when we consider the mode of that instruction, which is overwhelmingly oral: "Laura would *call* the little ones / And *tell* them," "Would *talk* about the haunted glen," and so forth (548–49, 552; my emphases). The substance of this oral transmission is manifestly the same as that of the five-hundred-line poem we have just been reading, whose antically irregular rhymes breathe a nursery air, and whose supple, frisky metrics practically have to be sounded out, in the mind's ear if not aloud, in order to catch their distinctive, spontaneous music. To be sure, the ambiguous position of the epilogue, coming after the story it depends on yet also operatively commands, makes it impossible to equate the third-person narrative voice with Laura's. Besides, as an oral storyteller Laura has a bardic license to tell her oft-told tale different ways at different sittings, in contrast to the fixity of the one printed text before us.

At least one hopes she tinkers a bit with her vocabulary: to imagine the circle of little ones puzzling over terms in the text like *pellucid, purloin, obstreperously,* and *succous pasture,* a thesaurus-tripper's periphrasis for *juicy food*—to imagine the kids reacting to this gilt-edged diction is to shake off the spell of a naive orality. It is to recall, that is, how Rossetti, like other Victorian pioneers in children's literature, was at work in a compromised mode that owed its charm to the ways it played reading against listening. The text as a whole invites us to imagine such a performance as publisher Alexander Macmillan staged when he read out "Goblin Market," shortly before publication, to a skeptical yet eventually enthralled "working-man's society," or again, such a performance as the poet herself apparently conducted when reading aloud to fallen women at the shelter in Highgate where she volunteered.[5] The text invites us not just to *read it,* but to *read it to ourselves,* to let it talk us into a mode of virtual orality. And virtual orality, I shall argue, has everything to do with the economic thematics of Rossetti's story.

Much of my argument will be found implied, by the reading ear, in the poem's opening lines:

Morning and evening
Maids heard the goblins cry:
"Come buy our orchard fruits,
Come buy, come buy...."
(1–4)

The phrase "Come buy" recurs more than a dozen times in "Goblin Market" as the "iterated jingle" (253) of a straightforward sales pitch. Yet a vigilant virtual orality has to wonder how to take it. How is the imagined listener to know what the reader so plainly sees, that "buy" has a letter *u* in the middle of it—to know that the goblins are not freely offering something (Do come by our orchard some time) but rather selling something for a price? The listener *in the poem* knows what's up, right away and beyond any doubt: the first thing said by either of the maids who hear the goblins cry is that "We must not buy their fruits" (43). That our country maids thus know just what they are hearing is as sure a sign as any in the poem that they are conscious denizens of a market economy, where the way to come by a nice piece of fruit is to come and buy it; where "Come buy" betokens not hospitality but trade. The verbal confusion here is all ours, the virtual listeners'; this happens, I submit, because Rossetti wants us to read verbal confusion as cultural confusion. Embedded (or endeared, as John Keats might say) within the reigning order of contract and purchase, she invites us to recognize an older order of invitation and gift, which mercantilism has on one hand superseded as clearly as literacy has superseded orality, yet which on the other hand mercantilism has less abolished than engrossed, for rhetorical purposes, as a hidden persuader.[6] About this kind of subliminal promotion Rossetti's market-wise maids seem clueless: Lizzie means to reinforce her sister's "We must not buy" when she declares, "Their *offers* should not charm us, / Their evil gifts would harm us" (65–66; my emphases); but the way her declaration confounds purchase with donation, confounds the boughten with the given (via the ambiguously *offered*), would do a politician proud. And this confusion discloses something about the promotional strategy that underwrites the goblins' deceptively straightforward "Come buy."

NOTES

1. See, inter alia, Dorothy Mermin, "Heroic Sisterhood in *Goblin Market*," *Victorian Poetry* 21 (1983): 107–18, and Helena Michie, "'There Is No Friend Like a Sister': Sisterhood as Sexual Difference," *ELH* 56 (1989): 401–21; Mary

Arseneau, "Incarnation and Interpretation: Christina Rossetti, the Oxford Movement, and *Goblin Market*," *Victorian Poetry* 31 (1993): 79–93, and Linda E. Marshall, "'Transfigured to His Likeness': Sensible Transcendentalism in Christina Rossetti's 'Goblin Market,'" *University of Toronto Quarterly* 63 (1994): 429–50; Paula Marantz Cohen, "Christina Rossetti's 'Goblin Market': A Paradigm for Nineteenth-Century Anorexia Nervosa," *University of Hartford Studies in Literature* 17 (1985): 1–18, and Deborah Ann Thompson, "Anorexia as a Lived Trope: Christina Rossetti's 'Goblin Market,'" *Mosaic* 24 (1991): 89–106; David F Morrill, "'Twilight Is Not Good for Maidens': Uncle Polidori and the Psychodynamics of Vampirism in *Goblin Market*," *Victorian Poetry* 28 (1990): 1–16; Shelley O'Reilly, "Absinthe Makes the Tart Grow Fonder: A Note on 'Wormwood' in Christina Rossetti's *Goblin Market*," *Victorian Poetry* 34 (1996): 108–14; Paula Bennett, "'Pomegranate-Flowers': The Phantasmic Productions of Late-Nineteenth-Century Anglo-American Women Poets," in *Solitary Pleasures: The Historical, Literary, and Artistic Discourses of Autoeroticism*, ed. Paula Bennett and Vernon A. Rosario II (New York, 1995), 189–213.

2. Elizabeth Campbell, "Of Mothers and Merchants: Female Economics in Christina Rossetti's 'Goblin Market,'" *Victorian Studies* 33 (1990): 393–410; Terrence Holt, "'Men Sell Not Such in Any Town': Exchange in *Goblin Market*," *Victorian Poetry* 28 (1990): 51–67; Elizabeth K. Helsinger, "Consumer Power and the Utopia of Desire: Christina Rossetti's 'Goblin Market,'" *ELH* 8 (1991): 903–33; Richard Menke, "The Political Economy of Fruit: *Goblin Market*," in *The Culture of Christina Rossetti: Female Poetics and Victorian Contexts*, ed. Mary Arseneau, Antony H. Harrison, and Lorraine Janzen Kooistra (Athens, Oh., 1999), 105–36.

3. Lorraine Kooistra, "Modern Markets for *Goblin Market*," *Victorian Poetry* 32 (1994): 249–77.

4. Christina Rossetti, "Goblin Market," lines 468–71, from *The Complete Poems of Christina Rossetti*, ed. R.W. Crump, vol. 1 (Baton Rouge, 1979), hereafter cited parenthetically by line number in my text.

5. Alexander Macmillan to Dante Gabriel Rossetti, 28 October 1861, quoted in *The Rossetti–Macmillan Letters*, ed. Lona Mosk Packer (Berkeley, 1963), 6–7. Jan Marsh, *Christina Rossetti: A Literary Biography* (London, 1994), 218–38, stresses the Highgate Penitentiary connection.

6. John Keats, "Ode on a Grecian Urn," line 13, in *Complete Poems*, ed. Jack Stillinger (Cambridge, Mass., 1978). Subliminal allusion alert: this phrase comes from Vance Packard's popular exposé of subliminal advertising, *The Hidden Persuaders* (New York, 1957).

—Herbert F. Tucker. "Rossetti's Goblin Marketing: Sweet to Tongue and Sound to Eye." *Representations* 82, spring 2003: 117–120.

[Winston Weathers is Professor Emeritus of English at the University of Tulsa. In his career he established himself as a scholar of Victorian Poetry, and he has published many articles on Christina Rossetti.]

Christina confesses herself, in her allegory, "A Royal Princess," a great awareness of self.

> All my walls are lost in mirrors, whereupon I trace
> Self to right hand, self to left hand, self in every place,
> Self-same solitary figure, self-same seeking face.

And in these lines she confesses not only an awareness of self, but of fragmented self, for the phrase, "self to right hand, self to left hand," suggests the dichotomy of personality into differing, if not antithetical, forces.

These forces of the self Christina allegorizes in her poems dealing with sisterhood. The various sisters which appear in her work are the mythic characters in her psychological drama, and such poems as *Goblin Market*, "A Triad," "The Queen of Hearts," "Sister Maude," "Noble Sisters," and many others provide her commentary on the varying actions and interactions which occur within the inner being. Time and time again, Christina brings two sisters together—sometimes three—in moments of crises, letting them debate with one another, struggle with one another, in mythic action that illustrates both a subtle understanding of self on Christina's part and a tragic realization of fragmentation that belies the calm, serene exterior that Christina presented to the world. Not recounting real experience, not revealing homosexual predilections, the sister poems are simply Christina's discussion of psychological truths which she witnessed in herself and which are universally significant in that all our personalities are subject to an analysis into parts, whether we call those parts "the brothers and sisters of our soul" or, with Freud, the ego, superego, and id.

The prototypal poem in Christina's myth of the self is, of course, *Goblin Market*. In this early and most famous poem, Christina creates her essential characters—Laura and Lizzie—and moves them through a drama that leads from innocence and integration to sickness and fragmentation back to a newer and more mature balance, represented in part by the marriage of the sisters and their assumption of marital responsibility. One need not identify the two sisters and the goblins too precisely in order to recognize the resolution that occurs. That the two sisters are aspects of one self is evident when they are described as being "like two blossoms on one stem" and "locked together in one nest," yet that they are different from one another is evident in their very actions. Laura, whose "restraint is gone" and Lizzie, who is "full of wise upholdings," respond in their different ways to the goblins who parade before them. The goblins, obviously, are some state of mind, some mental experience that is both attractive and destructive, both exotic and visionary at the same time it is immensely real. One would not go too far astray, it seems, to recognize in the goblins and their wares a kind of imaginative, fanciful, visionary—even hallucinatory—state of mind that is escape from reality, beautiful escape at the same time it is intellectually destructive. To see in the goblins simply the sexual or the sensuous is to limit their role in Christina's myth and limit their function. No doubt sex and sensuality are there, but other mysterious regions of the mind and of the self also exist that lure one to psychological death. The whole fairy-tale machinery, the animal shapes of the goblins suggest what a bizarre nature the goblin experience was to Christina herself and suggest whole inexplicable areas of detachment from reality.

Such Nietzschean terms as Apollonian and Dionysian may help us understand the fundamental drama of *Goblin Market*. The different phases of human nature which Laura and Lizzie represent are similar to those Nietzsche recognized, principally in *The Birth of Tragedy*, as eternal polarities of self, the one, the Dionysian, leading to tragedy, the other, the Apollonian, leading to survival. The Dionysian aspect of self is pulled strongly toward the whole ritualistic fulfillment that Laura experiences with the goblins, while the Apollonian self holds back from the make-believe, the visionary and ritualistic "reality" in preference for a more logically-oriented reality, a more objective, exterior world. Not that Lizzie is unaware of the goblins and that potential state of mind. The whole self is aware of the goblins. But whereas one part of self surrenders to illusion and an essentially intensional accommodation to life, the other part of self struggles to maintain a distance from the deep, archetypal, even primordial freedom and makes, in turn, an essentially extensional accommodation to existence.

Laura comes near her death in surrendering to a myth that can be imagined from afar but which cannot be accepted as a replacement for reality. Stepping into that state of mind which the goblins represent, Laura finds herself in that pathological state which modern psychiatry has dealt with so extensively and which is, indeed, a deep illness. All of Laura's symptoms following her purchase of the goblin fruit are those of the mentally ill. Withdrawing from reality into that illusion of the goblins, Laura finds herself in that pitiful trap of having lost contact with one reality only to find its supposed replacement to be air and vacancy. Lizzie, the remaining fragment of the whole self, must now struggle to integrate again, to become one whole person again, and to do this she must face up to the very illusory state of mind—the goblin market—that is the "snake pit" for Laura. In sound psychiatric fashion, Lizzie re-enacts the goblin experience, meets it face to face in a kind of therapeutic recognition, without actually succumbing to it, and by doing so is able to pull Laura back from the brink.

—Winston Weathers. "Christina Rossetti: The Sisterhood of Self." *Victorian Poetry* vol. III, 1965: 81–83.

TERRENCE HOLT ON THE FORCES AT WORK IN THE POEM

[Terrence Holt has published "'Men Sell Not Such in Any Town': Exchange in Goblin Market".]

In *The Madwoman in the Attic*, Sandra Gilbert and Susan Gubar observe that Christina Rossetti's *Goblin Market* has become a "textual crux for feminist critics" (p. 566). Gilbert and Gubar themselves see in it a bitter renunciation of literature—of an art, they argue, that is (and perhaps can only be) male.[3] More recently, Dorothy Mermin has described *Goblin Market* as an assertion of women's literary power. The two readings seem impossibly opposed, suggesting that another, unacknowledged, force is at work within the text, a force that neither reading sees whole.

One such force within *Goblin Market* is economic. Economic language and metaphors, terms of finance and commerce ("buy," "offer," "merchant," "stock," "money," "golden," "precious," "sell," "fee," "hawking," "coin," "rich," etc.) permeate the poem, which opens with an extended invitation to the market: "Morning and evening / Maids heard the goblins cry: / 'Come buy our orchard fruits, / Come buy, come buy.'"[4] The phrase "come buy" echoes throughout the poem, its iteration stressed by the description of it as the goblins' "shrill repeated cry" (l. 89), their "customary cry, / 'Come buy, come buy,' / With its iterated jingle / Of sugar-baited words" (ll. 231–234). Economic metaphors inhabit apparently innocent words: the cry is "customary" because it solicits the custom of Lizzie and Laura; the words "jingle" not only because of their iteration,[5] but because they evoke the jingle of coin (cf. ll. 452–453). That the goblins are costermongers, economic creatures as well as sexual ones, suggests that sexual and economic systems of relation may intersect in other ways as well.[6]

Despite the pervasiveness of the goblins' cry, however, the ostensible function of this discourse of the marketplace is to stress the difference between maidens and goblins. Exchange, *Goblin Market* claims, is the province of goblins, not of girls. Indeed, Lizzie and Laura seem to know instinctively that "We must not look at goblin men, / We must not buy their fruits" (ll. 42–43). The market is dangerous to maids, who belong safely at home. This emphasis on difference is of course partly a matter of sexual difference. But this is not so much an interest in the prurient possibilities of difference as an attempt at keeping the sexes apart. A separation between maidens and goblins must be preserved, the poem warns, because commerce with goblins is dangerous to maids. The goblins' glen is "haunted" (l. 552), and has caused the death already of one maid (ll. 147–161). Lizzie's virtuous horror of the place (ll. 242–252) alludes to a nameless threat, but her delicate evasion only pretends to conceal the obvious: the threat is the proverbial fate worse than death.

The sexual threat in the glen touches as well on another concern in *Goblin Market*, the place of women in the literary world. The glen echoes with a literary tradition that has used women as sexual scapegoats. The "bowers" (l. 151) from which these fruits are plucked parody a similar snare in Spenser, the Bower of Bliss; Laura's reaction to this low, swampy place (ll. 226–227) suggests its affinity with the Slough of Despond in *The Pilgrim's Progress*.[7] A woman who enters the glen, especially a woman writer, places herself in a historical context that assigns her a negative value on the literary exchange.

A difference between maidens and goblins must be preserved, furthermore, because commerce with the goblins is also potentially infectious: the threat in the goblins' glen is not only that one may be attacked by them; but that one may become like them. Their victims become as "restless" (l. 53) as the brook that whispers there, a restlessness like the "Helter skelter, hurry skurry" (l. 344) activity that typifies the goblins. Lizzie, counseling her sister to keep away, assumes that separation can enforce difference, an assumption echoed in the two passages that introduce us to the sisters' home.

Home in *Goblin Market* seems the opposite of the goblins' glen, isolated from the world of commerce. The first scene in the home (ll. 184–198) stresses the sisters' isolation, in implicit contrast to the goblins' prolific trade. The home is also a scene of busy industry, wherein the sisters produce healthful foods independently of the marketplace, foods that differ pointedly from the goblins' exotic fruits:

> Early in the morning
> When the first cock crowed his warning,
> Neat like bees, as sweet and busy,
> Laura rose with Lizzie:
> Fetched in honey, milked the cows,

Aired and set to rights the house,
Kneaded cakes of whitest wheat,
Cakes for dainty mouths to eat,
Next churned butter, whipped up cream,
Fed their poultry, sat and sewed;
Talked as modest maidens should:
Lizzie with an open heart,
Laura in an absent dream,
One content, one sick in part;
One warbling for the mere bright day's delight,
One longing for the night. (ll. 199–214)

The sisters produce foods for their own consumption, enacting on an economic level the hermeticism of their domestic scene. The description of the sisters as they set to work compares them to bees, and the simile is peculiarly apt: they are bee-like not only in the quiet hum of their industry, but especially in their self-sufficiency, producing with their own labor the food that sustains them.

The sisters themselves glean from nature the raw materials of food they produce at home, and have no need to resort to the market to trade for someone else's wares. By contrast, the goblins' wares may not even have been, originally, their own. Lizzie's question about their fruit—"Who knows upon what soil they fed / Their hungry thirsty roots?" (ll. 44–45)—questions the root-origins of those fruits; the goblins have the look of middlemen, and their fruits, coming from a tropic distance, seem far from their native soil. This goblin capital is thus doubly alienated, an alienation that makes the sisters' apparently uncomplicated and direct nourishment by the land yet another sign of their difference from the commercial goblins.

The repeated journeyings back and forth between market and home make this difference literal, defining a physical distance between them. The two are separated by an extensive waste (l. 325), a steep bank (l. 227), and a gate (l. 141). The goblins themselves stress the difference between the two places in their conversation with Lizzie, who wants to take some of their fruit back to succor her dying sister: "Such fruits as these / No man can carry; / Half their bloom would fly" (ll. 375–377), they tell her. Indeed, the failure of the "kernel-stone" to grow goblin-fruit at the sisters' home (ll. 281–285) reinforces their message. The two places belong to different biological (and moral) orders, a difference that, despite Laura's despair, is ultimately consoling: if that kernel had grown, what havoc might its fruit have wrought in the sisters' domestic haven?

But the repeated distinctions between the glen and the home, which seem intended to assert the sisters' independence from goblin economics, are not as absolute as they seem. The home is inescapably involved in economics—as the word's Greek root, *oikonomia* ("management of a household"), suggests. The domestic is historically a scene of economic exploitation, prison and workhouse as much as haven.[8] *Goblin Market* expresses the potential involvement of the home in exchange in part by the very strength of its attempt to evade such involvement.[9]

The insistence on the separation between the two realms cannot conceal the home's contamination by exchange. Even in our first view of it, Laura already keeps house in an "absent dream," "sick in part" and "longing for the night" (ll. 211–214). She only seems like a modest maiden; inside, the goblin's poison is working in her veins. The honey they gather is tainted: it has appeared already in the poem, literally in a goblin's mouth. "In tones as smooth as honey" (l. 108), the goblins hawk their wares to the sisters. The honey not only sustains the home but is at the same time an inducement to go outside it, to partake in the system of exchange that invades and undoes that world.

NOTES

3. Gilbert and Gubar, p. 575. For phallogocentrism see Jacques Lacan, *Ecrits: A Selection*, trans. Alan Sheridan (New York, 1977), pp. 281–291; Jane Gallop, *Reading Lacan* (Ithaca,1985), pp. 133–156; Luce Irigary, *Speculum of the Other Woman*, trans. Gillian C. Gill (Ithaca, 1985), pp. 13–129; Shoshana Felman, "Women and Madness: The Critical Phallacy," *Diacritics* 5, no. 4 (1975): 2–10, and "Rereading Femininity," *YFS* 62 (1981): pp. 19–44; and Mary Jacobus, *Reading Woman* (New York, 1986), pp. 83–196, esp. pp. 110–136.

4. Christina Rossetti, *Goblin Market*, in *The Complete Poems of Christina Rossetti*, ed. R.W. Crump (Baton Rouge, 1979), 1:11–26, ll.1–4. All further quotations from this edition appear parenthetically by line number within the text.

5. For the role of iterability in linguistic circulation, see Jonathan Culler, *On*

Deconstruction: Theory and Criticism after Structuralism (Ithaca, 1982), p. 102.

6. See Catherine Gallagher, "More about 'Medusa's Head,'" *Representations* 4 (Fall, 1983): 55–57, for discussion of costermongers as emblems of eighteenth- and nineteenth-century anxieties about economic and gender roles.

7. Spenser's villainesses typify the monstrous-feminine as defined in Julia Kristeva, *Powers of Horror: An Essay on Abjection*, trans. Leon S. Roudiez (New York, 1982), pp. 1–31; the rhetoric of scum, filth, and blood in Bunyan's description of Christian's family as well as the Slough draws heavily on the religious vocabulary Kristeva also identifies (pp. 56–89) with the "holy abject."

8. Gilbert and Gubar, p. 570; see also pp. 122–126, 134–137, 171–180, 289–291, 381, 382, 545, 558–559, and Mary Poovey, *The Proper Lady and the Woman Writer: Ideology As Style in the Writings of Mary Wollstonecraft, Mary Shelley, and Jane Austen* (Chicago, 1984), pp. 3–47.

9. For discussion of the futility of such evasions see: Sigmund Freud, "The Uncanny," in *The Standard Edition of the Complete Psychological Works of Sigmund Freud* (London, 1953–74), 17:219–252; Jacques Derrida, "The Law of Genres," *Glyph* 7 (1980): 202–232; and Michel Foucault, *History of Sexuality* (New York, 1980), 1:1–50.

—Terrence Holt. "Men sell not such in any town": Exchange in *Goblin Market*. *Victorian Poetry* vol. 28, no. 1, spring 1990: 51–54.

MARY ARSENEAU ON SYMBOLIC INTERPRETATION

[Mary Arseneau is an Associate Professor in the Department of English at the University of Ottawa. She is the co-editor of *The Culture of Christina Rossetti: Female Poetics and Victorian Contexts*. She has also written articles on John Keats and Dante Alighieri.]

If we place *Goblin Market* within the larger context of Rossetti's thoughts on religion, poetry, and symbol, we will find that certain fundamental habits of thought evident throughout her writing can help us to understand *Goblin Market* as a paradigm of the kind of symbolic interpretation in which Rossetti wanted her readers to engage. The importance of Lizzie and Laura's attempts to interpret their experiences in the poem can be better appreciated by reading *Goblin Market* in light of Rossetti's own statements on the ways in which the individual should respond to the beauty and temptations that the world offers. In this regard, it is crucial that we recognize that one of the most fundamental assumptions underlying Rossetti's poetry is her theologically based belief that the created world is capable of communicating moral and spiritual meaning, or, in her own words, that "All the world over, visible things typify things invisible."[2] There were several influences in Rossetti's life that would have encouraged this belief, but by far the most important was the impact of the intense incarnationalism and sacramentalism of the Oxford Movement.

Critics have often noted that Rossetti first came under the influence of the Oxford Movement in 1840, and that by 1843, when thirteen years of age, she had begun regularly attending the High Church services at what Canon Henry W. Burrows calls "the leading church" in the Oxford Movement at that time— Christ Church, Albany Street.[3] I would like to pursue this formative connection further by considering the influence that Tractarian habits of thought had on Rossetti's conceptions of symbolism and interpretation and by demonstrating how Rossetti's understanding of symbolism sheds important light on Goblin Market. The Tractarians saw the incarnation as the vital core of the Church, its sacraments, and God's plan for humanity's redemption.[4] In addition to this intense incarnationalism, the Tractarians were known for their sacramentalism, a term which refers both to their reverence for the sacraments of the Church and to the broader concept of their awareness of the transcendent as sacramentally and analogically present in the material world and in human life. This belief was not lost on Rossetti: as Raymond Chapman observes, the Oxford Movement deeply affected Rossetti's habits of thought by teaching her that "the visible and invisible worlds were not sharply separated" (p. 194). In Rossetti's poetry and prose this belief is manifested in her consistent emphasis on the need to read things and events in a spiritual light.

The Oxford Movement's influence on Rossetti, moreover, extended beyond the strictly theological. In *Victorian Devotional Poetry: The Tractarian Mode*, G.B. Tennyson examines the wide influence that Tractarian poetry and poetics had on the sensibilities of the Victorian age, and in his postscript he delineates briefly the necessity and advantages of seeing Rossetti as an inheritor of Tractarian poetics. Indeed, there is ample evidence that she was familiar with the poetry of such prominent Tractarians as John Henry Newman, Isaac Williams, and John Keble;[5] but by far the most important evidence of Rossetti's contact with Tractarian poetics is a copy of John Keble's extraordinarily popular and influential volume, *The Christian Year*.[6] In her copy of this book Rossetti marked certain titles in the table of contents, highlighted numerous passages with vertical lines in the left margin, underlined individual lines, and drew in the top margins a pencil illustration to accompany each poem.[7] Given this evidence, it is imperative that we consider what Rossetti might have absorbed from her study of Keble.[8]

According to Keble, God had originally created human beings as belonging at once both to the natural and supernatural worlds. However, as a result of original sin, the direct link between the human and the supernatural world was severed; the world ceased to be an image of the supernatural and became instead a mere shadow of it. According to Keble, postlapsarian nature was restored by the incarnation and by Christ's sacrifice, which made nature a sacramental symbol of the divine. Christ's incarnation is thus the source of the analogy which is central to Keble's poetic. However, in the time since the incarnation, the material world has become "much more alluring for its own sake" (Beek, p. 78), and the result is that people have been blinded to the symbolic meaning of the material world. Through God's gift of grace, the moral sense, which has been clouded by sin, is restored. This moral sense is inseparable from the "symbolic sense" in Keble's philosophy; the moral sense leads the individual to God, but only because the symbolic sense enables him or her to see the symbolic representations of the supernatural world within the physical world that God has created.

As her copy of *The Christian Year* demonstrates, Keble's sacramental aesthetic was noted by Rossetti. Diane D'Amico states that "the most obvious distinction between marked and unmarked stanzas is that the marked ones could all be spoken by Rossetti herself";[9] but more importantly, an examination of Rossetti's copy also reveals that she often marked passages describing the emblematic, educative, and sacramental qualities of creation. The following marked lines clearly refer to the ongoing presence of Christ in the world:

There's not a strain to Memory dear,
    Nor flower in classic grove,
There's not a sweet note warbled here,
    But minds us of Thy Love.
O Lord, our Lord and spoiler of our foes,
There is no light but Thine: with Thee all beauty glows.
                     ("Third Sunday in Lent," ll. 49–54)

Through the ongoing effect of the incarnation Christ's presence informs earthly beauty; the duty then falls on the Christian to search for Christ in this world and to attempt to understand the world in terms of Christ and the incarnation. Rossetti notes these following lines that counsel the Christian to look for Christ in everything: "Let not my heart within me burn, / Except in all / Thee discern" ("Evening," ll. 23–24).

For Rossetti, the profoundly spiritual possibilities of symbolism in poetry and nature are enabled by the descendental motion of a God who makes Himself available to humankind, especially through that central Christian event and symbol, the incarnation. Rossetti conceives of the incarnation as working on many levels to bridge the gap between the material world and a higher, spiritual one: in the person of Christ, divinity and humanity coexist; in the sacramental system instituted by Christ, and in particular in the Eucharist, divine grace becomes available through a physical form; and through the incarnation establishes a principle of analogy between the earthly and the divine, making nature the symbol of the divine and forging a link between the spiritual and the physical. But Rossetti also emphasizes that the human consciousness must transcend the material world, an action which complements the descendental motion enacted by God. The link between heaven and earth is thus similar to Jacob's ladder with its continuous and simultaneous ascending and descending motion (Genesis 28.12). The transcendental movement is realized in the interpretative acts of the individual (whether a character in a poem or the reader of it) who attempts to give a moral and symbolic reading to things and events, and who in doing so attempts to look through the physical toward an analogous spiritual realm. Rossetti is advocating this mode of perception in this passage from her commentary on the Ten Commandments, *Letter and Spirit*:

> We should exercise that far higher privilege which appertains to Christians, of having "the mind of Christ;" and then the two words, visible and invisible, will become familiar to us even as they were to Him (if reverently we many say so), as double against each other. (p. 131)

For Rossetti, such penetrating interpretation is enabled by a consciousness of the spiritual, for without spiritual discernment there can be no real understanding of the natural and material. She emphasizes in *Seek and Find: A Double Series of Short Studies of the Benedicite*:

> Thus we learn that to exercise natural perception becomes a reproach to us, if along with it we exercise not spiritual perception. Objects of sight may and should quicken us to apprehend objects of faith, things temporal suggesting things eternal. (p. 180)

The natural world has an important part to play in Rossetti's theology and aesthetics, for while she recognizes it as a lesser good than the heavenly reward to which she aspires, this world remains an important avenue to God. We learn about God through His creation, and we work toward our own salvation according to how we think and act in this world. But Rossetti (like Keble) is also extremely wary of the physical world, worried that the attractions of the material and sensory can distract the individual from the higher purpose of achieving salvation. According to Rossetti, the world must be constantly subordinated to the heavenly reward: "It is good for us to enjoy all good things which fall to our temporal lot, so long as such enjoyment kindles and feeds the desire of better things reserved for our eternal inheritance" (*Seek and Find*, p. 180). This world is beautiful and good, but only if it serves as a stepping stone to help the individual know and love God; as Rossetti writes to her brother William Michael's future wife, Lucy Madox Brown,

"When earth is an anteroom to heaven (may it be so, of God's mercy to us all), earth itself is full of beauty and goodness."[10] But Rossetti also often worried that the material world is capable of leading one away from God:

> O LORD Jesus Christ, King for ever and ever, suffer not the kingdoms of the world or the glory of them to enslave any heart from Thy free service. Let not the worldly influence sway us, or worldly glory dazzle us, or this vain life enthrall us in its shadow, or riches weigh us down to earth, or pleasure slay us. Amen. (*Annus Domini*, p. 40)

Typically, despite her great appreciation for natural beauty, Rossetti is suspicious that what is appealing to the senses can also be dangerously capable of distracting one from proper priorities.

In attempting to reconcile, on the one hand, her desire to see the world as a sign of God and, on the other, her fear that in loving the world too much a person can become blind to spiritual realities, Rossetti achieves a poetically and spiritually satisfying balance between the two through the use of natural images which comprehend the appeal of physical beauty while dedicating the physical to her higher purpose of explaining how the material world must be transcended: "This is not my orchard for fruit or my garden for flowers. It is however my only field whence to raise a harvest" (*The Face of the Deep*, p. 333). This image of the harvest, with its rich biblical echoes,[11] is a seamless merging of natural and spiritual fruition and resounds throughout *Goblin Market and Other Poems*, from the harvest scene of the title poem that signals Laura's spiritual renewal[12] to the highly evocative gathering of sheaves in the final poem:

> It is over. What is over?
> Nay, how much is over truly:
> Harvest days we toiled to sow for;
> How the sheaves are gathered newly,
> Now the wheat is garnered duly. ("Amen," ll. 1–5)

Rossetti often explicitly tells her readers to search for spiritual messages in the natural world, but in a more "reserved" way (to use a Tractarian term) her highly symbolic use of natural images also acts as a model of how necessary it is to read all natural things for the deeper symbolic meanings they convey. The harvest image is typical of Rossetti's symbols in its effortless wedding of the natural image with religious meaning; in doing this it embodies the meaning and method of Rossetti's symbolism.

In *Goblin Market*, the sisters Lizzie and Laura both hear the goblin men's tempting offers of luscious fruit. Lizzie rejects the fruit as "evil," while Laura is tempted and indulges. After eating the goblin fruit, Laura's health and peace of mind deteriorate; and Lizzie realizes that she must procure some of the goblin fruit in order to save her sister's life. Lizzie goes to purchase the fruit; she refuses to eat with the goblin men who torment her and try to force her to eat, but she manages to withstand and then runs home to Laura, who is cured by tasting the juices smeared on Lizzie's face. Many critics have regarded temptation as the thematic core here, but even more fundamental to the poem is the problem of the interpretation of things and events, the task of giving things a right moral reading; and Keble's description of the "symbolic sense" as one of the moral sense's "constituent elements" (Beck, p. 78) helps clarify why the ability to read symbolically plays an integral role in Lizzie's, Laura's, and the reader's moral interpretation of things and events in the poem. Any symbolic and moral reading in and of *Goblin Market* necessarily must grapple first with the meaning of the goblin fruit. Many critics have seen the goblin fruit as the forbidden fruit of sexual sin; however, as D'Amico points out in "Eve, Mary, and Mary Magdalene: Christina Rossetti's Feminine Triptych," when Rossetti considers the first human sin, Eve's eating of the forbidden fruit, she does not interpret it in sexual terms: "For Rossetti, Genesis was primarily a warning against disobedience, not lust."[13] The passage from *Letter and Spirit* that D'Amico cites shows that Rossetti considered Eve's sin to be in her preferring "various prospects to God's will" and diverting her "'mind' ... from God Almighty" (p. 179). Bearing this in mind, we may do well to look in *Goblin Market*, not for evidence of a sexual fall, but for evidence of a turning away from God.

NOTES

2. *Seek and Find: A Double Series of Short Studies of the Benedicite* (London, 1879), p.309. *Seek and Find* was the second of Rossetti's six volumes of devotional prose, preceded by *Annus Domini* (London, 1874) and followed by *Called to be Saints* (London, 1881), *Letter and Spirit* (London, 1883), *Time Flies* (London, 1885), and *The Face of the Deep* (London, 1892). Subsequent references to these works will be cited in the text with title and page number.

3. Henry W. Burrows, *The Half-Century of Christ Church, St. Pancras, Albany Street* (London, 1887), p. 14. For the most full treatments to date on Rossetti's connection to the Oxford Movement, see G.B. Tennyson, *Victorian Devotional Poetry: The Tractarian Mode* (Cambridge, Massachusetts, 1981); Raymond Chapman, *Faith and Revolt: Studies in the Literary Influence of the Oxford Movement* (London, 1970); the final chapter of Katherine J. Mayberry, *Christina Rossetti and the Poetry of Discovery* (Baton Rouge, 1989); and Diane Apostolos-Cappadona, "Oxford and the Pre-Raphaelites from the Perspective of Nature and Symbol," *JPRS* 2 (1981–82): 90–110.

4. Eugene R. Fairweather, *The Oxford Movement* (New York, 1964), p. 14.

5. A catalogue of *Books from the Libraries of Christina, Dante Gabriel, and William Michael Rossetti* indicates that Christina's library contained a rare first edition of Newman's *The Dream of Gerontius*, published in 1866 ([London, 1973], p. 27). Rossetti's first biographer, MacKenzie Bell, tells us that Rossetti also had a great regard for the Tractarian poet Isaac Williams, author of *Thoughts in Past Years, The Cathedral, The Baptistery, The Altar*, and of two important tracts, "On Reserve in Communicating Christian Knowledge" (*Christina Rossetti: A Biographical and Critical Study* [Boston, 1898], p. 184); and we have the supporting evidence of an 1881 letter to Dante Gabriel, in which she quotes Williams approvingly, saying the quotation "is a couplet (Isaac Williams) I thoroughly assent to" (*The Family Letters of Christina Georgina Rossetti*, ed. William Michael Rossetti [London, 1908], p. 103). We also know that when she was writing *Seek and Find*, she consulted Isaac Williams' *A Harmony of the Four Evangelists* (1850).

6. John Keble, *The Christian Year: Thoughts in Verse for the Sundays and Holydays Throughout the Year*, 16th ed. (Oxford, 1837). All subsequent references will be cited in the text with poem title and line number. I would like to thank Susan Rossetti Plowden and Stephen Plowden for their generosity in allowing me to study this volume.

7. Diane D'Amico suggests that we can infer from the presence of these illustrations that the book was being studied and illustrated by Rossetti during the late 1840s, "for during that time she began to show an interest in developing any artistic talent she might have had and in using that talent to illustrate poetry." Furthermore, a poem copied onto one of its blank pages indicates that Rossetti was still using this book frequently after 1859, and one of Rossetti's marginal notes indicates that she was reading *The Christian Year* sometime after 1866 ("Christina Rossetti's *Christian Year*: Comfort for the Weary Heart," *VN* 72

[Fall 1987]: 36, 41); thus, there can be no denying that Rossetti did give *The Christian Year* considerable attention and returned to it over an extended period of time.

8. W.J.A.M. Beek's *John Keble's Literary and Religious Contribution to the Oxford Movement* (Nijmegen, 1959) provides a good overview of Keble's theological and poetical position.

9. D'Amico, p. 40.

10. *The Family Letters of Christina Georgina Rossetti*, p. 39.

11. For example, Christ's parable of the wheat and the tares in Matthew's Gospel specifically identifies the sowing of good seed and its due harvest with the heavenly reward: "The Kingdom of heaven is likened unto a man which sowed good seed in his field" (13.24). But in the parable an enemy, whom Christ identifies as the devil (13.39), secretly plants tares among the wheat. At harvest time the tares are picked and burned (the hellish punishment of the wicked) while the sheaves of wheat are gathered into the barn. When seen in this context, the image of the harvest involves a theme ever present in Rossetti's life and poetry: the need to make oneself worthy of salvation. Moreover, in the Bible, this image of the harvest is specifically linked with the need to work toward a spiritual reward: "for whatsoever a man soweth, that shall he also reap. For he that soweth to his flesh shall of the flesh reap corruption; but he that soweth to the Spirit shall of the Spirit reap life everlasting" (Galatians 6.7–8).

12. *Goblin Market*, ll. 530–542. All quotations from Rossetti's poetry are from *The Complete Poems of Christina Rossetti*, ed. R.W. Crump, 3 vols. (Baton Rouge, 1979–90). Subsequent references will be cited in the text.

13. Diane D'Amico, "Eve, Mary, and Mary Magdalene: Christina Rossetti's Feminine Triptych," in *The Achievement of Christina Rossetti*, ed. David A. Kent (Ithaca, 1987), p. 179.

—Mary Arseneau. "Incarnation and Interpretation: Christina Rossetti, the Oxford Movement, and Goblin Market." *Victorian Poetry* vol. 31, no. 1, spring 1993: 79-84.

CATHERINE MAXWELL ON THE FRUITS OF ROSSETTI'S IMAGINATION

[Catherine Maxwell is Senior Lecturer in the Department of English and Drama at Queen Mary, University of London. Her most recent work is *The Female Sublime from Milton to Swinburne* and she has also written articles on Browning and Thomas Hardy.]

Sandra M. Gilbert's reading of *Goblin Market* offers a useful parallel to my proposed reading because it also sees the poem as allegory, though in this case it is an allegory of limitation. For Gilbert, the poem pictures the woman writer who wishes to experience the full fruits of her imagination, but Rossetti, too much bound by conventions, is unable to let herself or her female characters have this freedom. Rebellious Laura must suffer for her impetuosity when she gives in to her desire to eat the goblin fruit. However, prudent Lizzie intervenes to save her sister and restore her to the safe but conservative sphere of home. The focus in this reading is as much on the initially conflicting desires of the sisters as on the encounters with the goblin men. Nonetheless, the reading as a whole is supported by a wealth of allusions to men's texts and patriarchal traditions. The biblical story of the Fall in Genesis, Milton's retelling of this story in *Paradise Lost*, the New Testament narrative of Christ's temptation, and the Eucharistic liturgy are identified as underlining the poem's moral message about temptation and redemption, its "bitter repressive wisdom." Gilbert also cites Keats's poem "La Belle Dame Sans Merci" as an analogy to (rather than an influence on) *Goblin Market*, but while she sees Keats's poem as daring advocacy—"Art ... is ultimately worth any risk"—she roundly condemns Rossetti's poem for playing safe.

While Gilbert's allegory does not specify direct male sources for the poem, it does identify the goblins with male precursors:

> the goblin men ... are of course integrally associated with masculinity's prerogatives of self-assertion, so that what Lizzie is telling Laura (and what Rossetti is telling herself) is that the risks and gratifications of art are not "good for maidens," a moral Laura must literally assimilate.... Young ladies like Laura ... and Christina Rossetti should not loiter in the glen of imagination, which is the haunt of goblin men like Keats and Tennyson—or like Dante Gabriel Rossetti and his compatriots of the Pre-Raphaelite Brotherhood.

Furthermore the allegory associates the goblin fruits with the literary imagination: "works of art—the fruits of the mind." Laura is seen as "metaphorically eating *words*." Gilbert never quite declares that these artful verbal fruits are poems. I would propose that not only are they poems but that they are men's poems. The fruit is directly identified as goblin produce ("goblin fruits"). Its flesh and juice, described as "Goblin pulp and goblin dew" (470), suggest that it partakes of the same bodily nature as the goblin men, that it is a synecdoche for the goblins' own fleshly, masculine, and potent juices. However, Rossetti evokes multiple echoes that connect the fruits not only with masculinity but with male-owned or male-identified texts.

The most fundamental references are biblical. The scriptures not only belong to a venerable patriarchal tradition, they are also regarded by Protestants as the Word of God, authored by his Holy Spirit. The forbidden fruit consumed by Eve in Genesis is the exclusive property of the paternal Creator God. This fruit, which confers knowledge of good and evil, has the capacity to make the partaker intellectually powerful like God who, recognizing the threat of usurpation, ejects the disobedient human couple from Eden before they gain immortality by eating from the Tree of Life (Gen. 4:22). Human beings are punished for eating God's fruit, but in the New Testament they are actively encouraged to redeem themselves and have "eternal life" by ingesting the Word of God as embodied in Christ. Christ's redeeming blood, symbolized by wine, revives Old Testament fruit imagery, as does his claim to be "the true vine" (John 15:1). Fruit and the male body are also connected in the Old Testament Song of Solomon. Most modern readers would read the Song simply as an erotic poem but, in the interpretation traditionally approved by ecclesiastic authority, the Song is a spiritual allegory of Christ's relationship to his Bride, the Church, conveyed through a series of sensual love lyrics. At the beginning of the Song, the female speaker identifies her lover with apple trees and their fruit—fruit that will satiate her longing for him. "As the apple tree among the trees of the wood, so is my beloved among the sons. I sat down under his shadow with great delight, and his fruit was sweet to my taste. He brought me to the banqueting house, and his banner over me was love. Stay me with flagons, comfort me with apples: for I am sick of love" (Song 2:3–5). These biblical texts form a web of associations which connect fruit with male authority and knowledge as well as with the male body and its potency.

But Rossetti is also trading on the associations formed by the male poetic tradition. Milton, often seen as the father of modern poetry, launches the figure of potent fruitfulness into English verse when he retells the story of the Fall in *Paradise Lost*. Milton's serpent enlarges on the Biblical serpent's tempting promise "ye shall be as gods" (Gen. 3:5) in a flood of eloquence, declaring that the tree's fruit has not harmed but rather empowered him. Impressed by the evidence that the fruit "Gave elocution to the mute," Eve succumbs to temptation and eats the "intellectual food." Milton's emphasis on the superior powers of articulation bestowed by the fruit, powers exercised by Eve immediately after eating, strengthen the links between fruit and verbal artistry. Like Eve who returns home to try out her persuasive speech on Adam, fallen Laura returns to Lizzie, meeting her sister's reproachful warnings with a paean in praise of the banquet she has just consumed. Her language, notably more elaborate than anything previously voiced by the maidens, now directly imitates the goblin men's persuasive cries, but it is also infiltrated by Romantic poeticisms such as "pellucid," "odorous," "mead," and "velvet." She continues her oral gratification by filling her mouth with verbal evocations of the pleasure-giving fruit that has stimulated both her physical appetite and her love of language.

Milton describes the Tree of Knowledge as infused with "sciential sap, derived / From nectar, drink of gods." This inspiring, honey-sweet juice, the sap of Edenic forbidden fruit, seeps into the writings of his male followers, where it is imbibed by Rossetti. In Keats's "La Belle Dame Sans Merci," the faery's seduction of the knight-at-arms involves a bewitching song and enchanted foods—"roots of relish sweet, / And honey-wild, and manna dew." Rossetti revises Keats's "faery's song" into the goblins' "iterated jingle / Of sugar-baited words" (233–34) and "tones as smooth as honey" (108), and glamorizes Keats's sweetmeats into an altogether more exotic collection of fruits, which seduces the reader as much as it does Laura. However, the glamour she imparts to them is partly derived from other

Keatsian texts such as "The Eve of St. Agnes" (30.265–70) where luscious fruits are an aid to seduction. Keats's more earthy "roots" (and thus some of the roots of Rossetti's poem) are preserved in Laura's ingenuous question about sources—"Who knows upon what soil they fed / Their hungry thirsty roots?" (44–45)—and Keats's knight, stricken as he is, nonetheless offers us and Rossetti an example of the powers of the creative imagination under enchantment.

Coleridge's visionary youth in "Kubla Khan" is also drunk with his inheritance from Milton: "For he on honey-dew hath fed, / And drunk the milk of Paradise," and Tennyson, too, experiences the enticement of the sap "liquid gold, honeysweet" which fills the closely guarded apples of "The Hesperides" ("The luscious fruitage clustereth mellowly, / Goldenkernelled, goldencored / Sunset ripened") and the sedative enchanted fruits of "The Lotos-Eaters." Both these Tennyson poems are about the allure of poetic imagination. The first and earlier poem defends the place of the imagination, founded on its likeness to Milton's Eden, against all who try to rob it of its fruitfulness. The second poem reminds us of "The Palace of Art" with its admonitions about the poet isolating himself from the "real" world, but the actual recreation of Lotos-land is dreamily evocative enough for us to understand it as a temptation.

Rossetti, allured by the visions of her male predecessors, is an intruder in the Hesperean garden of English poetry. Her goblin men and goblin fruits are her way of indicating a tradition of male-authored poems that use fruit, fruit-juice, and honey-dew as motifs for imaginative inspiration and poetic influence, and her poem shows how women poets can claim their place in this tradition by appropriating this "sciential sap" for themselves through theft. In this, *Goblin Market* resembles the strategies of female authorship discussed by Patricia Yaeger in her book *Honey-Mad Women*, which employs the image of honey stealing and drinking to illustrate the woman writer's relationship to the male tradition.

Yaeger cites passages from a poem by the American poet Mary Oliver in which a "she-bear," who stands in for the female writer, steals honey to illustrate "the seriously playful, emancipatory strategies that women writers have invented to challenge the tradition." She comments: "In Oliver's 'Happiness' we meditate upon the female poet's good appetite; her possession of language is equated with the possession of a delicious excess of meaning that is forbidden, but therefore twice delicious. Once found it lightens the speaker's clamorous burden of feeling." While Rossetti's forbidden fruits with their "delicious excess" of sexual, economic, religious, and intertextual meanings offer an excellent analogy to Yaeger's allegory, Yaeger's treatment of appropriation is much more idealized than Rossetti's:

> The scenes that Mary Oliver depicts in her poem are such scenes of theft: we may recall Derrida's insistence that the *"letter,* inscribed or propounded speech, is always stolen.... It never belongs to its author or to its addressee." Oliver reproduces the female writer's pleasure in discovering this ownerlessness, in lightening the fictions that weigh her down, in stealing and incorporating the languages that, until she claimed them, did not belong to her.

Although the letter may always be stolen, this does not mean that the female writer sees it as "ownerless." Part of her difficulty in negotiating with a male literary tradition is that poetic language, even though it may always be without an ultimate author or owner, *seems* very much a male property, although this can also increase her pleasure in stealing. Yaeger tends to simplify the difficulties of theft, but she does usefully note that "male language" can also be represented by women as a poison, as dangerous. She cites Monique Wittig's *Les Guérillières,* but we might also think of those fruits "like honey to the throat / But poison in the blood" (554–55). Yaeger picks up this last reference in her own treatment of *Goblin Market,* but her discussion of the poem is surprisingly brief and marred by the fact that she confuses Lizzie with Laura. She uses the poem as a personal allegory of the dangers and pleasures experienced by the woman critic drawing upon male theory: "I would like to argue, as Laura implicitly does, that this gathering of male texts can also represent a feminist harvest." While this is true, Yaeger misses the opportunity of seeing the whole poem as a commentary on women's dangerous yet necessary relation to the male literary tradition.

Rossetti's poem reveals that women cannot enter this tradition on the same footing as men, any more than they can compete with men on equal terms in the mid-Victorian marketplace. Yet it also suggests that female interaction with the male tradition, however complicated and risky, is inevitable. Although the goblins are presented as dangerous creatures to be outwitted and escaped, they also give this poem its motivating energy. In other words, the goblins and the need to conquer them are necessary, as the poem charts a typical path from innocence to experience. The goblin fruits are also the fruits of experience, but Rossetti shows women learning to control that experience in order to maintain their own fruitfulness. (One thinks of another of her poems, "An Apple Gathering," which warns against the risk of picking flowers too early and thus losing the chance of fruit.) Women poets need to develop different strategies to avoid being overpowered by male influence to the extent that they can no longer write poems of their own. Trying to buy the goblins' fruit, Laura compromises herself by giving away part of her female identity—her golden curl. When she subsequently dines on the goblins' fruit; she loses all taste for her home-produced food, and from this we might infer that an exclusive diet of male texts seems to starve the female literary imagination. But Lizzie, like a woman poet who realizes she cannot simply buy into the male tradition, is resistant to the blandishments of the goblins, refusing to swallow their sales pitch. Rossetti's depiction of goblin aggression writes in what is missing from Gilbert and Gubar's account, as the woman struggles with or resists her male precursors. Resistance means that Lizzie obtains the fruit-juice surreptitiously without paying for it; she steals rather than buys. Following her own intuition she knows that if she takes away the juice *on* rather than *in* her body, she can transform it into something of her own—"my juices" (468). Like many readers, the Victorian poet Alice Meynell was puzzled by the different effects of the fruit juice, writing that "we miss any perceptible reason why the goblin fruits should be deadly at one time and restorative at another." But in a poem that is all about sources, context becomes all important. Given by the goblin men, the fruit juice is like a poison, but mediated by a loving, sister, sucked from a woman's body, it becomes a restorative antidote.

—Catherine Maxwell. "Tasting the 'Fruit Forbidden.'" *The Culture of Christina Rossetti: Female Poetics and Victorian Contexts*, eds. Mary Arseneau, Antony H. Harrison, and Lorraine Janzen Kooistra. Athens: Ohio University Press, 1999: 80–85.

RICHARD MENKE ON THE MATERIALITY OF THE POEM

[Richard Menke is an Assistant Professor in the Department of English at the University of Georgia. He has also written articles on Henry James and George Eliot.]

If more than a century of critical response is any guide, Christina Rossetti's *Goblin Market* would seem to remain as delicious and mystifying as the goblin fruit it describes. In response to the speculations it provoked, Rossetti herself claimed that the poem was only a fairy story, utterly without "any profound or ulterior meaning," but notwithstanding her pronouncement, *Goblin Market* has remained the subject of innumerable interpretations, especially religious, psychological, and biographical ones. Artless children's story or sophisticated allegory, unconscious fantasy or carefully crafted fable, *Goblin Market* does in fact possess the texture of a fairy tale, with its singsong repetitions, its mingling of the mundane with the outré, its curious mixture of otherworldliness and acute materiality. Indeed, this materiality is one of its most memorable and attractive, even seductive, qualities. I wish to consider the materiality of the poem, especially as it centers around representations of fruit as physical object and commodity, and to offer a reading of the poem that brings Rossetti's so-called "aesthetics of renunciation" into line with what I consider her sharp but subtle economic critique— that is, to read Rossetti's renunciatory poetics alongside Victorian political economy, the "science of *wealth*" that is "simultaneously the science ... of want, of *thrift*, of *saving*," of "*asceticism*" and "[s]elf-denial": the science of renunciation.

Terrence Holt has complained that most contemporary readings of *Goblin Market* emphasize "the goblins, and the issues of sexuality and gender they seem to represent," at the expense of "the market," but recently several accounts of the poem have attempted to redress the situation. Holt himself discusses *Goblin Market* in terms of the various patterns of exchange—linguistic, psychological, economic, and sexual—that structure it. Elizabeth Campbell draws upon the work of Julia Kristeva to examine the interaction of gender and market relations in the poem's contrast between male linearity and female cyclicality. Working from Nancy Armstrong's claim that "the 1860s represent a new moment in the history of desire in which consumer culture changed the nature of middle-class femininity," Mary Wilson Carpenter considers the double way in which the poem treats women's bodies as "consumable," that is, both as able to be consumed and destroyed by men, and as sustaining and life-generating. By focusing on the shadow figure of the prostitute, Elizabeth K. Helsinger explores *Goblin Market*'s treatment of the relationship between women and the marketplace, and incisively questions the poem's ultimate utopian solution to the problems this relationship presents. But if *Goblin Market* is indeed a poem about consumers and markets, what might goblin fruit—its central representation of the consumable and marketable—mean?

The *OED* traces the movement of the word *fruit* through its centuries of use in English: from its core meaning of physical botanical product, to its biblically inflected extension into metaphor ("the fruit of the righteous is a tree of life," "the fruit of the womb"), and finally to a point where the metaphorical again becomes material (fruit as the result of labor, fruit as financial profit). In a curious way, the motion of *Goblin Market* itself parallels and reiterates the movement of *fruit*, its drift from the physical to the metaphorical and back to the physical, and does so, I argue, largely through the lavishly described yet always mysterious "goblin fruit" itself. Inspired first of all by the long list that foregrounds the goblin fruit, and even the words used to represent the fruit, as sensuous and firmly particular, the first sections of this essay consider the fruit of the goblin market as fruit in the mid-Victorian market. My emphasis then shifts to the metaphorical or metonymic meanings of the goblin fruit, especially in terms of dominant Victorian political economy and John Ruskin's attempts to rewrite economics along aesthetic and ethical lines. Finally, the essay attempts to re-materialize the fruit in order to interrogate its imaginary status as the realization of that abstract concept, a "commodity," and by doing so, to recapture the poem's critical power—and to recognize its crucial equivocations.

UNSEASONABLE FROSTS

Such a reading of *Goblin Market* must begin by defining the site of the poem's production, locating it not merely discursively but also spatially and temporally, finding its starting point before tracing its trajectory. Indeed, this site seems intriguingly antithetical to the imaginary setting of the poem. In place of a picture-book countryside we have London (in which Christina Rossetti spent most of her life, and about which she wrote few of her poems); in place of fairy-tale timelessness, a particular year and even a specific day: April 27, 1859, the date written on the manuscript.

It was an unusual spring in England, to say the least, and one that had followed an unusual winter. An 1859 article in *Turner and Spencer's Florist, Fruitist and Garden Miscellany* compares the mild English winter just past to one in "the south of Italy." In the wake of such a warm season, Christina Rossetti might well have anticipated that the coming spring would be a green and pleasant one. If she did, she must have been terribly disappointed, for after this uncommonly gentle winter, the "extraordinary vicissitudes" of English weather soon proved disastrous to the trees and flowers she loved and wrote about. In fact, these vicissitudes seem exceptionally likely to have decisively affected the composition, possibly even the original conception, of *Goblin Market*. The *Florist's* writer continues:

> Very early in February a number of shrubs were fast breaking into leaf, and Apricots opening their blooms; during March all went on unchecked, so much so, that ... the woodlands and pasture

grounds presented all the appearances usually shown by the first week in May, and every description of garden produce partook also of the general earliness of the season.

But these early blossoms and fruit, like Jeanie's "gay prime" in *Goblin Market*—and almost like Laura's "early prime"—come to an end when a frost brings premature destruction (316, 549):

> On the 31st of March we had 10° of frost, which, following after a snow the previous evening, did a vast amount of mischief to such fruit trees in bloom, besides destroying, in several places the crops of Apricots, which were then of considerable size. Peaches had partly set, and suffered more or less throughout the country; and early Pears and Plums also.

Even at this point, one gardener notes the many plants lost and the "fruit trees shorn of promising crops." But the unusual conditions continue:

> The weather became warmer, and the 4th, 5th, 6th, and 7th of April were remarkable for their great heat, the day temperature having been 82° in this neighborhood on the 7th, and between 70° and 80° the greater part of the former three days, an extraordinary temperature for the first week of April.... The weather next became sensibly colder, and on the 14th and following days indications of winter made their appearance, followed by snow storms, cold north-west winds, and frosty nights. On the morning of the 10th we had 8° of frost, accompanied by an easterly wind; this frost has almost completed the ruin of our crops of Pears, Plums, and Cherries, excepting perhaps those in some favored locality, or which had ample protection, things almost impossible to effect within the means of an ordinary garden expenditure, to say nothing of orchards and open garden fruits.

Another writer notes the results of this "most disastrous" frost in more detail:

> Apricots were a most abundant crop on the walls, and as large as Damsons. On trees unprotected, or protected only with nets, every fruit is destroyed; on trees protected with tiffany, even

double, some few are left, perhaps one in 1000, but these, although green and apparently sound, have their kernels brown and dead. Peaches and Nectarines under the same circumstances seem all destroyed; they had set an immense crop. I never remember them blooming more kindly or setting their fruit better, owing to their shoots being so well ripened by the warmth of the summer and autumn last year. Some few kinds of Plum were in full bloom ... the germs of all the expanded blossoms are destroyed.... Pear trees here had not unfolded their blossoms, but they seem to have suffered much.

After the abundant harvests and well-supplied fruit market of the preceding seasons, in the spring of 1859 Britain seemed likely to grow precious little fruit in the coming season. One gardener in Lincolnshire reports the loss of all his peaches, and many of his gooseberries, currants, pears, and both early and late apples. A Yorkshire correspondent to the *Gardeners' Chronicle and Agricultural Gazette* notes the widespread lamentation over the recent weather's effect on the British fruit crop: "Expectations of abundant crops are blighted, and now the cry is that the severe frosts of the last two days of March and the greater part of April have all but destroyed our fruit." No doubt, nearly everyone in England in the spring of 1859 would have been painfully conscious of the extremely intemperate weather between the end of March and late April, but further awareness of the resulting state of British fruit was hardly restricted to a handful of disappointed fruiterers writing in horticultural magazines. The *Economist's* weekly account of foreign goods on the British market outlines the increasing scarcity of lemons and oranges, some of the most popular varieties of fruit for importation, from the end of March to the end of April. On April 23 it reports a "[m]arket bare of oranges," a week later one emptied not only of oranges but now also of lemons. By May 7, the "backward season for fruit of home growth" seemed "likely to clear the market of foreign produce" as well, as Britons substituted imported for homegrown fruit. Anyone in England who sought a sweet orange to eat or wanted a lemon for punch would very likely have had to do without. Given the destruction of the new fruit crop and the subsequent scarcity of imported fruit, England in late April 1859 must have been a particularly fruit-less place.

According to the manuscript of *Goblin Market*, Christina Rossetti completed the poem or at least wrote out this most important draft on April 27, 1859. Even if the unhappy situation of British horticulture and the fruit trade did not positively determine the representation of the conspicuously plentiful and luscious fruit in *Goblin Market*, it cannot help but have informed it. In place of a "renunciatory aesthetics" that simply and unquestioningly spurns present pleasures, here perhaps is a poetics that takes genuine enjoyment in displacing absence, or at least one acutely sensitive to the dynamic relationships between desire and constraint, pleasure and imagination. The fulfillment of such desires, the realization of such pleasures, may depend on the consumption of goods, but poetic imagination may provide a substitute—or may make the ache of desire more acute. If the inventory of fruit in *Goblin Market* seems dreamlike in its intense physicality, the reasons for this paradox may in fact be legitimately historical: at the time the poem was written, fresh fruit would indeed have been largely the stuff of fantasy. In the context of a real market barren of lemons or oranges, of orchards with apricots, pears, peaches, and cherries dead on the boughs, how great must have been the sheer extravagance, and perhaps the level of denial, involved in producing such a fantastic catalogue. Or how great must have been the power of such a call as the goblin men incessantly make to their prospective customers. "Morning and evening / Maids heard the goblins cry," begins *Goblin Market* (1–2). The poem then proceeds to mimic its goblins by articulating their cry, a marvelously encyclopedic and paratactic call that includes twenty-nine kinds of fruit in twenty-nine lines:

> "Come buy our orchard fruits,
> Come buy, come buy:
> Apples and quinces,
> Lemons and oranges,
> Plump unpecked cherries,
> Melons and raspberries,
> Bloom-down-cheeked peaches,

Swart-headed mulberries,
Wild free-born cranberries,
Crab-apples, dewberries,
Pine-apples, blackberries,
Apricots, strawberries;—
All ripe together
In summer weather,—
Morns that pass by,
Fair eves that fly;
Come buy, come buy:
Our grapes fresh from the vine,
Pomegranates full and fine,
Dates and sharp bullaces,
Rare pears and greengages,
Damsons and bilberries,
Taste them and try:
Currants and gooseberries,
Bright-fire-like barberries,
Figs to fill your mouth,
Citrons from the South,
Sweet to tongue and sound to eye;
Come buy, come *buy*." (3–31)

"Bloom-down-cheeked peaches," "Figs to fill your mouth"—
it certainly seems a list to fill one's mouth, exquisitely "sweet to
tongue and sound to eye"; simply to read the list aloud is almost
to "taste them and try." In another poet, in another poem, the
effect of the cry's penultimate line might be to give a whiff of
synaesthesia, mere sensory shift. But here, language and food,
sight and taste, the visual and the auditory and the physical
("sound to eye") all begin to merge. The combination will soon
prove dangerous to Laura, for whom "a peep at goblin men"
seems almost automatically to entail trafficking with them and
consuming their fruit (49). The power of the fruit and the power
of the merchants' language overlap in this visionary introductory
catalogue. And in its sheer profusion, the list works at least
temporarily to keep things in the realm of the material, to
"overload the senses and ... impair the observer's ability to see
beyond the physical."

—Richard Menke. "The Political Economy of Fruit." *The Culture of Christina Rossetti: Female Poetics and Victorian Contexts*, eds. Mary Arseneau, Antony H. Harrison, and Lorraine Janzen Kooistra. Athens: Ohio University Press, 1999: 105-111.

LORRAINE JANZEN KOOISTRA ON THE POETIC FANTASY

[Lorraine Janzen Kooistra is Chair of the Department of English at Nipissing University in Ontario, Canada. Her recent publications include *Christina Rossetti and Illustration: A Publishing History* and *The Culture of Christina Rossetti: Female Poetics and Victorian Contexts*, co-edited with Mary Arseneau and Antony H. Harrison.]

Christina Rossetti's best-known poetic fantasy, *Goblin Market*, is a work of immense visual power, employing a figural language both richly evocative and suggestively vague. With its mixture of the erotic and the religious, the social and the moral, the childlike and the profound, *Goblin Market* has always been a potent inspiration for illustrators. From 1862 to the present, *Goblin Market* has sparked the imaginations of at least eighteen artists, each of whom has responded to the poem's intriguing indeterminacies with pictorial representations designed to fix Rossetti's fantastic subject by reifying her metaphors. These illustrated editions offer us a range of "visual 'positions'" for Rossetti's fantasy in cultural contexts extending from the Pre-Raphaelite to the postmodern. The interaction between Rossetti's Victorian text and the images that have been produced to accompany it provides a fruitful study in cultural poetics, for visual depiction, as Gordon Fyfe and John Law observe, "is never just an illustration.... [I]t is the site for the construction and depiction of social difference. To understand a visualisation is thus to inquire into its provenance and into the social work that it does ... to note its principles of exclusion and inclusion, to detect the roles that it makes available, to understand the way in which they are distributed, and to decode the hierarchies and differences that it naturalises. And it is also to analyse the ways in which authorship is constructed or concealed and the sense of audience is realised."

Illustrations have the power to visualize Rossetti's poetic fantasy for a variety of audiences in a range of historical times and places. The implications of this power extend well beyond a single poem's history of production and reception to include the larger question of the role of visual culture in identity formation generally; as W.J.T. Mitchell demonstrates in *Picture Theory*, "the tensions between visual and verbal representations are inseparable from struggles in cultural politics and political culture." Thus, in order to understand the "social work" performed by illustration, it is indeed necessary, as Fyfe and Law suggest, to interrogate the ways in which roles are constructed, hierarchies and differences established, and audiences realized. My focus in this study of *Goblin Market*'s cultural production from the mid-nineteenth century to the present is on the ways in which feminine subjectivity has been visualized in contexts ranging from fine art books to children's picture books to pornographic magazines. "What is at stake" here, as Rosemary Betterton argues in *Looking On: Images of Femininity in the Visual Arts and Media*, "is the power of images to produce and to define the feminine in specific ways." Indeed, visual culture demands investigation because it is one of the "defining and regulatory practice[s]" by which sexualities are represented, produced, mediated, and transformed. In a work such as *Goblin Market*, whose subject matter turns on the pleasures and transgressions of looking as they relate to the formation of female subjectivity and identity, pictures of women and goblins present spectacles of fantasy and femininity that are neither passive nor innocent. Rather, they have the power to compete with the text for the dominant representation of the story. By visualizing metaphor, artists construct critical lenses through which readers view Rossetti's fantasy. Thus image and text are engaged in a dialogue in which two ways of looking at femininity, and two ways of encoding that vision, are presented to the reader. The dialogic relations between picture and word enact a struggle between spectatorship and spectacle which mirrors *Goblin Market*'s own engagement with the conflicting (and conflicted) positions of looking and being looked at.

In illustrated versions of *Goblin Market* the identity of the subject is constructed along a split axis of visual and verbal images in a way that parallels bath the conflicted consciousness of Rossetti herself and the split subjectivity of her female subjects, Lizzie and Laura. As feminists from Simone de Beauvoir onward have noted, feminine subjectivity entails a divided consciousness: a woman is simultaneously aware of her self as an independent ego and her self as object. A woman's awareness of her self as "Other" is constructed both through the gaze of the male subject who has the power to perceive and manipulate objects, and through the reciprocal, coopted consent of the woman who "must pretend to be an object." Following feminist theories of the gaze, Dolores Rosenblum has written powerfully about Rossetti's own double awareness of herself as active creative agent and passive artistic model, noting that in *Goblin Market* Rossetti overcomes "the dualism between the 'active' see-er and the 'passive' seen" to the extent that "the model transcends the artist, and the spectacle for all eyes becomes the witness" of Lizzie's restorative actions of watching and rescuing. The transcendence Rosenblum assigns to Rossetti's text, however, is part of the poet's utopian fable, and is limited to her own production of the poem as verbal narrative. When her text is reproduced in illustrated editions, the poet loses authorial control, and the fantasy becomes a collaborative enterprise—a cultural commodity whose production and reception are determined by the imaginative vision of artists and the audiences for whom their images are constructed.

Rossetti's poem contests the traditional paradigm whereby "pleasure in looking ... [is] split between active/male and passive/female" with her recuperation and celebration of not only the female spectator, but also the redemptive function of woman *as* spectacle. However, many of the visual images that have been produced to illustrate *Goblin Market*'s themes have offered the more familiar story of feminine subjectivity in relation to visual pleasure. Some of these visualizations redirect the subversive energy of the poem by representing Lizzie and Laura as passive objects of the gaze; others comment critically on the text by providing images of female resistance and struggle; all construct the feminine when they compose their fantastic subjects. If Rossetti's poem asserts the need for women to be engaged with their world as lookers and doers, the illustrations have the power to transform these active female heroes into objects to be looked at, still images of beautiful otherness. Readers of illustrated *Goblin Market*s are thus frequently faced with two ways of looking at the same story, and their reading of Rossetti's narrative is mediated by the dialogue between the poetic fantasy and the visual object. For this reason, I will begin by examining the text's attitude to looking before moving on to investigate the ways in which Rossetti's fantasy has been offered to the gaze of its readers in illustrated editions.

Looking at Rossetti's Poetic Fantasy

Goblin Market is a poem that turns on women's relation to looking and being looked at. Rossetti's initial title for the poem— "A Peep at the Goblins"—focuses on its scopophilic themes. While at first blush the word "peep" may evoke the innocent playfulness of her cousin Eliza Bray's *A Peep at the Pixies*, in the context of the narrative itself "peep" becomes overlaid with the connotations of furtive looking, stolen glances at the forbidden, clandestine curiosity. Both the feminine desire to look at the world and the prohibitions against it are established in the sisters' opening speeches. "We must not look at goblin men," says Laura, even as she is "pricking up her golden head" to get a better view. "You should not peep at goblin men," replies Lizzie, as she "cover[s] up her eyes, / ... lest they should look." Throughout the first half of the poem, Laura maintains her curiosity—her desire to see and experience—while Lizzie keeps her eyes deliberately closed to the wonders of the world: Laura "stare[s]," but Lizzie "dare[s] not look" (105, 243). The goblins and their luscious fruit become objects of Laura's gaze, sensuous emblems of her desire. She succumbs to temptation first because of what she sees and imagines and only secondarily because of what she tastes. When she can no longer hear the goblins' cries and is prohibited from buying more fruit, her first reaction is to feel "blind," not hungry (259). Her "sunk eyes" mirror her wasting subjectivity as she begins to see false mirages of her desire (288–92). At last Lizzie, who "watch[es] her sister's cankerous care" (300), becomes impelled to action, leaves her cottage for the haunted glen, "And for the first time in her life / [Begins] to listen and look" (327–28).

Venturing into the outside world means that Lizzie becomes a spectacle as well as a spectator: the goblins "spy" her at the very moment that she begins her furtive "peeping" (330) and immediately begin their visual seduction as they hold up dishes laden with fruit: "Look at our apples," they tell her, describing their wares in beautiful detail (352–62). Unlike Laura, however, Lizzie looks without succumbing to temptation; for her, the goblins and their fruits are not objects of desire, but means to an end. With her clear-sighted vision, Lizzie is able to recognize, as Laura was not, that the goblins' "looks were evil" (397). Thus, although the goblins viciously pummel her with their fruit, Lizzie resists them and triumphantly brigs home the restorative juices in syrupy streaks upon her face. When Laura kisses her, tastes the goblin juices, and falls into a fit that looks like death, Lizzie watches over her until Laura revives at dawn with her eyes clear and full of light, ready to see the world in new ways and to picture her experience for others in the language of story.

One of the lessons of *Goblin Market* is the visual/spiritual one of learning how to look and interpret correctly—to know that what seems fair may be foul: attractive goblin men betray; delectable fruits poison. This is certainly the lesson that Laura learns, and the one she passes on to the children at the end of the narrative. But Lizzie, too, learns something. She learns that a woman cannot live in the world without looking and being looked at. And she learns that, while these activities are paradoxically both destructive and redemptive, they are also essential to life, to love, to creativity. As a result of Lizzie's actions, Laura regains control over her selfhood; the sisters' relationship achieves a more intense level of love through their painfully acquired knowledge and power; and their experience is affirmed through the continuity of children and storytelling. In the course of their goblin encounters, Lizzie and Laura learn to look at themselves and each other in new ways, and to formulate alternate visions of female subjectivity.

Similarly, Rossetti invites her readers to contemplate the ways in which her hero, Lizzie, has the power to be both spectator and spectacle without forfeiting her individual subjectivity. In Christian terms, she can be "in the world but not of it"; in feminist terms, she can see men looking at her without becoming alienated from her own selfhood. In this way, the dynamics of looking in *Goblin Market* radically challenge the binary opposition between active male "see-er" and passive female "seen." Rossetti's fantasy posits a world in which women can take pleasure in looking and survive the ordeals of being looked at to emerge triumphant as storytellers who deliberately display themselves to the gaze of others as part of an exemplary spectacle—a redemptive image of feminine power and Christian virtue to be seen, understood, and imitated. Such a spectacle takes on special significance if we imagine Rossetti's ideal audience to be, as Jan Marsh posits, the girls and sisters at the Highgate Penitentiary for Fallen Women, where Rossetti was working as a lay sister when she wrote her poem.

Goblin Market is one of the many Victorian fairy tales whose alternate visions staged a social protest against the status quo by expressing a utopian desire for a better world. As Jack Zipes's groundbreaking work in the field suggests, these utopian tales had a characteristically "feminine, if not feminist" slant, not only because of their strong female protagonists, but also because of their emphatic suggestion "that utopia will not be just another men's world." The feminism of these fantasies—and Zipes specifically cites *Goblin Market* in this instance—involves "an intense quest for the female self." Many other readers of *Goblin Market* have seen precisely this kind of quest in the poem. Yet at the same time that Rossetti struggled to envision a female subjectivity encompassing action, desire, knowledge, and power, she was also constrained by the conventions of Victorian society, which constructed the feminine as passive, innocent, beautiful, and helpless. These were certainly the feminine virtues Rossetti herself conveyed when she modeled for the mother of God in two of her brother Gabriel's early works, *The Girlhood of Mary Virgin* and *Ecce Ancilla Domini*. As Rosenblum points out, Rossetti's dual experience as artist and model produced a split consciousness that is enacted in her poetry itself in "a range of seeing acts and visual 'positions.'" In trying to envision new ways of looking at women in *Goblin Market*, Rossetti both exploits and subverts the notion that women are objects of the gaze. Drawing on a religious rather than a carnal iconic tradition, Rossetti attempts to revision femininity by offering the story of Laura and Lizzie as an exemplary spectacle of strong and active womanhood.

—Lorraine Janzen Kooistra. "Visualizing the Fantastic Subject": Goblin Market and the Gaze. *The Culture of Christina Rossetti: Female Poetics and Victorian Contexts*, eds. Mary Arseneau, Antony H. Harrison, and Lorraine Janzen Kooistra. Athens: Ohio University Press, 1999: 137–142.

JEROME J. MCGANN ON RELIGIOUS ALLEGORY

[Jerome J. McGann is the John Stewart Bryan Professor at the University of Virginia and the Thomas Holloway Adjunct Professor at Royal Holloway College, the University of London. His publications include *Dante Gabriel Rossetti: The Collected Works* and *Byron and Romanticism*.]

'Goblin Market' is Rossetti's most famous poem, and certainly one of her masterpieces. The point hardly needs argument, for no one has ever questioned its achievement and mastery. What does need to be shown more clearly is the typicalness of 'Goblin Market' in Rossetti's canon—indeed, its centrality.

Though Rossetti herself declared that the work was not symbolic or allegorical, her disclaimer has never been accepted, and interpretations of its hidden or 'secret' meaning have been made from the earliest reviews. Everyone agrees that the poem contains the story of temptation, fall, and redemption, and some go so far as to say that the work is fundamentally a Christian allegory. Nor is there any question that the machinery of such an allegory is a conscious part of the work. 'Goblin Market' repeatedly alludes to the story of the fall in Eden, and when Lizzie, at the climax, returns home to 'save' her sister, the poem represents the event as a Eucharistic emblem (see especially lines

471–2). Other, less totalizing Christian topoi and references abound. The important 'kernel stone' (line 138) which Laura saves from the fruit she eats, and which she later plants unavailingly (lines 281–92), is a small symbolic item based upon the New Testament parable (see Matthew 7:15–20) about the fruit of bad trees; indeed, the entire symbology of the fruits is Biblical, just as the figures of the merchant men are developed out of texts in the book of Revelation (18:11–17).

Rossetti draws from this passage her poem's controlling ideas of the evil merchants as traffickers in corruption and of their fruits as deceptive and insubstantial. Consequently, an important key for interpreting the poem proves to be her own commentaries on the Revelation text. The commentary on verse 14 has a manifest relevance which can pass without further remark:

> *14. And the fruits that thy soul lusted after are departed from thee, and all things which were dainty and goodly are departed from thee, and thou shall find them no more at all.*

Or according to the Revised Version: 'And the fruits which thy soul lusted after are gone from thee, and all things that were dainty and sumptuous are perished from thee, and men shall find them no more at all':—reminding us of St. Paul's words to the Colossians: '... The rudiments of the world ... (Touch not; taste not; handle not; which all are to perish with the using)'.

As regards the second clause of the doom (*in this verse*), the two Versions suggest each its own sense. The Authorized, as if those objects of desire may have been not destroyed but withdrawn whilst the craving remains insatiable. According to both texts the loss appears absolute, final, irreparable; but (collating the two) that which *departs* instead of *perishing* leaves behind it in addition to the agony of loss the hankering, corroding misery of absence. (*Deep*, 421)

Her commentaries on verses 15–17 are equally pertinent. There the sacred text speaks of the coming desolation of Babylon, the merchant's city; Rossetti says of this event that, though it has not yet come to pass, it 'must one day be seen. Meanwhile we have known preludes, rehearsals, foretastes of such as this', and the thought leads her to her 'lamentation'. In this she cries 'alas' for those traditional political symbols of corruption (Sodom or Tyre, for example), but her lament builds to an interesting climax: 'Alas England full of luxuries and thronged by stinted poor, whose merchants are princes and whose dealings crooked, whose packed storehouses stand amid bare homes, whose gorgeous array has rags for neighbours!' (*Deep*, 422). Of course, Rossetti was no Christian Socialist (or even a Muscular Christian), and her chief concern here is not with the material plight of the socially exploited. Rather, she focuses on the material condition as a sign, or revelation, of an inward and spiritual corruption— Babylon, Tyre, Sodom, England—as in Tennyson and T.S. Eliot, these are all, spiritually, *one* city ('Unreal city'), the passing historical agencies of the recurrent reality of a spiritual corruption.

The Bible, both the Old and New Testaments, characteristically associates these 'Babylonian' corruptions with sensuality and sexual indulgence, and Rossetti uses this association in her poem. The goblin merchants tempt the two sisters with fruits that offer unknown pleasures, more particularly, with fruits that promise to satisfy their unfulfilled desires. The figure of Jenny is introduced into the poem partly to make plain the specifically sexual nature of the temptation and partly to show that the issues are intimately related to the middle-class ideology of love and marriage. Jenny's is the story of the fallen woman.

In this context, the final (married) state of the sisters might easily be seen as sanctioning the institution of marriage as the good woman's just reward. To a degree this is indeed the case; but 'Goblin Market' presents the marriages of Laura and Lizzie in such an oblique and peripheral way that the ideology of the marriage-as-reward is hardly noticed and is conspicuously deemphasized by the poem. The only men present in the story are the goblins, and Laura and Lizzie's emotional investments are positively directed toward women and children only. In fact, the poem's conclusion suggests that the sisters have made (as, it were) 'marriages of convenience', only, in 'Goblin Market', that concept has been completely feminized. It is as if all men had been banished from this world so that the iniquity of the fathers might not be passed on to the children. Hence we see why the only men in the story are goblin men: the narrative means to suggest, indirectly, that the men of the world have become these merchants and are appropriately represented as goblins.

The ultimate evil of the goblin merchants is that they tempt to betray, promise but do not fulfil. Indeed, they do not merely fail in their promises, they punish the women who accept these promises as true. Yet the power of their temptations does not come from the inherent resources of the goblins; it comes from the frustration of the women, which is represented in Laura's (and Jenny's) longings and curiosity. The goblins, therefore, tempt the women at their most vulnerable point, which turns out to be, however, the place of their greatest strength as well.

Here we approach the centre of the poem's meaning, the core of its paradoxical symbolism. The temptation of the goblins always turns to ashes and emptiness because it does not satisfy the women's fundamental desires (see Rossetti's commentary on Revelation 18:14 above). But in terms of the Christian allegory, this simply means that the goblins offer 'passing shows' to match what in the women are 'immortal longings'. Notice how tenderly Laura and Lizzie are presented together immediately after Laura's 'fall'; how she finally emerges from her experience completely unstained; how the poem turns aside, at all points, any negative moral judgement of her character; and how it does not read Laura's condition as a sign of her evil. Rather, Laura's suffering and unhappiness become, in the poem, a stimulus for feelings of sympathy (in the reader) and for acts of love (by Lizzie). These aspects of the poem show that, for Rossetti, the 'temptation and fall' do not reveal Laura's corruption but rather the nature of her ultimate commitments and desires, which are not—despite appearances, and were she herself only aware of it—truly directed toward goblin merchants and their fruits.

Laura's desires (they are 'Promethean' in the Romantic sense and tradition) are fulfilled in the poem twice. The first fulfilment is in the notorious passage at 464–74, which is as patently erotic and sensual in content as it is Eucharistic in form. The significance of this elemental tension becomes clear when we understand that the scene introduces a negative fulfilment into the work: Laura is released from the spell of erotic illusions ('That juice was wormwood to her tongue, / She loathed the feast' [lines 494–5]) and permitted to glimpse, self-consciously, the truth which she pursued in its illusive form:

> Laura started from her chair,
> Flung her arms up in the air,
> Clutched her hair:
> 'Lizzie, Lizzie, have you tasted
> For my sake the fruit forbidden?
> Must your light like mine be hidden,
> Your young life like mine be wasted,
> Undone in mine undoing
> And ruined in my ruin,
> Thirsty, cankered, goblin-ridden?'—
> She clung about her sister,
> Kissed and kissed and kissed her:
> Tears once again
> Refreshed her shrunken eyes,
> Dropping like rain
> After long sultry drouth;
> Shaking with anguish, fear, and pain,
> She kissed and kissed her with a hungry mouth.
> ('Goblin Market', lines 475–92)

This passage anticipates the poem's conclusion—the second, positive scene of fulfilment—where Laura tells the children the story of a sisterly love and bids them follow its example: 'Then joining hands to little hands / Would bid them cling together,— / For there is no friend like a sister' (lines 560–2, my emphasis). For passion and erotics are substituted feeling and sympathy, and for men are substituted women and children, the 'little' ones of the earth.

Thus we see how the Christian and Biblical materials—the images and concepts—serve as the metaphoric vehicles for understanding a complex statement about certain institutionalized patterns of social destructiveness operating in nineteenth-century England. As in so many of her poems, 'Goblin Market' passes a negative judgement upon the illusions of love and marriage. But the poem is unusual in Rossetti's canon in that it has developed a convincing positive symbol for an alternative, uncorrupted mode of social relations—the love of sisters.

This situation requires some further explanatory comment. In the story of Laura and Lizzie, we can observe patterns of conceptualization familiar from Rossetti's other works. One notes, for, example, that the goblins' power over women comes ultimately from the women's (erroneous) belief that the goblins have something which the women need, that the women are incomplete. Part of the meaning of 'Goblin Market' is the importance of independence, including an independence from that erroneous belief. Lizzie's heroic adventure on her sister's behalf dramatizes her integrity, her freedom from dependency on the goblins: she is not a relative creature but is wholly herself, and capable of maintaining herself even in the face of great danger.

Nevertheless, the premium which Rossetti placed upon personal integrity was always threatened by the demon of loneliness ('And left me old, and cold, and grey'). 'Goblin Market' turns this threat aside, principally via the symbol of sisterly love and the alternative socializing structures which that symbol is able to suggest and foster. An important formal aspect of the poem's resolution depends upon our awareness that Lizzie is not Laura's 'saviour', for this would simply represent a variant type of a dependency relationship. The true beneficiaries of the grace issuing from the events are 'the children', or society at large in its future tense.

So far as 'Goblin Market' tells a story of 'redemption', the process is carried out in the dialectic of the acts of both Laura and Lizzie. Laura behaves rashly, of course, but without her precipitous act the women would have remained forever in a condition of childlike innocence. Lizzie's timidity is by no means condemned, but its limitations are very clear. Laura's disturbed restlessness and curiosity suggest, in relation to Lizzie, an impulse to transcend arbitrary limits. But Laura's behaviour is the sign of her (and her sister's) ignorance and, therefore, of their inability to control and direct their own actions. When Laura 'falls', then, her situation reveals, symbolically, the problem of innocence in a world which already possesses the knowledge of good and evil. Where ravening wolves prowl about in sheep's clothing, the righteous must be at once innocent as the dove and cunning as the serpent. Lizzie's function in the poem, then, is to repeat Laura's history, only at so self-conscious a level that she becomes the master of that history rather than its victim. Still, as the story makes very clear, her knowledge and mastery are a function, and reflex, of Laura's ignorance and weakness. The definitive sign of their dialectical relationship appears in the simple fact that Laura is not finally victimized. She is only a victim as Jesus is a victim; she is a suffering servant. In a very real sense, therefore, the poem represents Laura as the moral begetter of Lizzie (on the pattern of 'The child is father of the man'). Lizzie does not 'save' Laura. Both together enact a drama which displays what moral forces have to be exerted in order, not to be saved from evil, but simply to grow up.

Laura and Lizzie, then, share equally in the moral outcome of the poem's events. The fact that their names echo each other is no accident—and who has not sometimes confused the two when trying to distinguish them at some memorable distance? Still, it makes a difference if one locates the poem's principal moral centre in Lizzie alone, as readers have always done. In fact, to have read the poem this way is to have read it accurately (if also incompletely); for Rossetti, as a morally self-conscious Christian writer, encouraged such a reading, as she wanted to do—for both personal and polemical reasons. She encouraged it because *that* way of reading the poem supports a Christian rather than a secular interpretation of the theme of independence. All readers of the poem will recognize its polemic against the women's dependence upon the lures of the goblin men; but from a Christian viewpoint, this polemic is based upon the idea that people should not put their trust in mortal things or persons, that only God and the ways of God are true, real, and dependable. Therefore, in the affairs of this world, the Christian must learn to be independent of the quotidian—translate, *contemptus mundi*—and come to trust in the eternal. So far as Lizzie seems a 'Christ figure'—a Eucharistic agent—'Goblin Market' argues for a severe Christian attitude of this sort.

But, of course, Lizzie seems something much more—and

much less—than a Eucharistic emblem, as Christina Rossetti well knew: she never placed 'Goblin Market' among her 'Devotional Poems'. Consequently, because Lizzie is primarily a 'friend' and a 'sister' rather than a 'saviour', the poem finally takes its stand on more secular grounds. Nevertheless, it uses the Christian material in a most subtle and effective way: to mediate for the audience the poem's primary arguments about love, marriage, sisterhood, and friendship.

In much the same way does the poem use the disarming formal appearance of a children's fairy story. This choice was a stroke of real genius, for no conceivable model available to her could have represented so well a less 'serious' and 'manly' poetic mode. When her publisher Alexander Macmillan first read the poem to a group of people from the Cambridge Working Men's Society, 'they seemed at first to wonder whether I was making fun of them; by degrees they got as still as death, and when I finished there was a tremendous burst of applause.'[17] All three phases of their response were acute. 'Goblin Market' cultivates the appearance of inconsequence partly to conceal its own pretensions to a consequence far greater than most of the poetry then being produced in more 'serious', customary, and recognized quarters.

Lizzie triumphs over the goblins (lines 329–463) by outplaying them at their own games, but one should notice that her victory is gained in and through her correct formal behaviour. It is the goblins who are violent, disorganized, out of control—and impolite. She addresses them as 'good folk' (line 362) and says 'thank you' (line 383) to their insidious offers. The goblins smirk and giggle at her apparent simple-mindedness, yet the poem clearly represents her as enjoying an unexpressed, superior laughter at their expense. Lizzie's behaviour is the equivalent, in 'Goblin Market', of what we spoke of earlier in relation to 'Winter: My Secret' and 'No, Thank You, John'.

Lizzie's behaviour is also a stylistic metaphor standing for Rossetti's poetry, whose correct beauty judges, particularly through its modest address, all that is pretentious and illusory. The fruits, the language, the behaviour of the goblin merchants are all metaphors for what Keats had earlier called 'careless hectorers in proud, bad verse'. The issues here are nicely suggested in a brief passage immediately following Lizzie's victory over the goblins: 'Lizzie went her way ... / Threaded copse and dingle, / And heard her penny jingle / Bouncing in her purse,— / Its bounce was music to her ear' (lines 448, 451-4). This is Rossetti's sign of a true poetic power—a mere penny which jingles like the surface of the verse. Nonsense (the original title of 'Winter: My Secret') and childishness—Edward Lear, Lewis Carroll, 'Goblin Market'—come into a great inheritance amid the fat and arid formulas of so much High Victorian 'seriousness'.

But 'Goblin Market' gains its results in the most obliging and diplomatic fashion. Christina Rossetti was a severe woman, and her ironic intelligence and quick tongue were observed, and respected, by all of her contemporaries who knew her. But so were her modest and retiring ways. She did not cultivate the weapons, or methods, of George Sand or even of Elizabeth Barrett Browning. Lizzie's behaviour with the goblins is Rossetti's poetic equivalent for her own life and work. What Lizzie does—what Rossetti does in her verse generally—is not to make a frontal assault upon her enemy, but quietly to secure his defeat by bringing righteousness out of evil, beauty out of ugliness. Rossetti's model for her revisionist project appears explicitly in her Revelation commentary cited above:

> Yet on the same principle that we are bidden redeem the time because the days are evil, Christians find ways to redeem these other creatures despite their evil tendency. Gold and silver they lend unto the Lord: He will pay them again. Precious stones and pearls they dedicate to the service of His Altar. With fine linen, purple, silk, scarlet, they invest His Sanctuary; and fragrant 'thyine' wood they carve delicately for its further adornment ... Whoso has the spirit of Elijah, though his horse and chariot have come up out of Egypt, yet shall, they receive virtue as 'of fire' to forward him on his heavenward course. And this despite a horse being but a vain thing to save a man. (*Deep*, 420)

Out of these convictions develop, naturally, the charming catalogues of the goblins as well as their own temptation speeches; but we recognize this habit of mind most clearly in the unspeakably beautiful litanies praising the poem's loving sisters:

> Golden head by golden head,
> Like two pigeons in one nest
> Folded in each other's wings,
> They lay down in their curtained bed:
> Like two blossoms on one stem,
> Like two flakes of new-fall'n snow,
> Like two wands of ivory
> Tipped with gold for awful kings.
> Moon and stars gazed in at them,
> Wind sang to them lullaby,
> Lumbering owls forbore to fly,
> Not a bat flapped to and fro
> Round their rest:
> Cheek to cheek and breast to breast
> Locked together in one nest.
> ('Goblin Market', lines 184–98)

Thematically this passage is important because of its position in the poem. Although the lines describe the evening rest of the sisters *after* Laura's encounter with the goblins, the passage does not draw any moral distinctions between Laura and Lizzie. In the perspective of Christina Rossetti's poem, Laura remains fundamentally uncorrupted. By goblin standards, she is now a fallen woman, but the poem intervenes to prevent the reader from accepting such a judgement.

This moral intervention occurs at the level of poetic form and verse style. As such, it does not merely tell us of the need for a new moral awareness, it suggests that this new awareness cannot be an abstract idea. On the contrary, it must operate in a concrete form appropriate to the circumstances—in this case, within the immediate literary event of the poem itself. The poem's general social critique (which is abstract) appears in the verse as a series of particular stylistic events (which are concrete). In a wholly non-Keatsian sense then, Beauty becomes Truth: not because the beauty of art represents a purified alternative to worldly corruptions, but because art's beauty is itself a worldly event, an operating (and, in this case, a critical) presence which argues that human acts will always escape, and dominate, what is corrupt.

NOTES

17. Alexander Macmillan to D.G. Rossetti, 28 Oct. 1861, quoted in *The Rossetti–Macmillan Letters*, ed. Lona Mosk Packer, Berkeley and Los Angeles, 1963, p. 7.

18. It is a commonplace of Rossetti criticism that her poetry is the best expression we have of the ideas and attitudes of Tractarianism. But this is a most misleading view (though not entirely wrong); one might rather turn to a work such as *The Christian Year* for an epitome of Tractarian ideology. Rossetti's evangelical sympathies kept her protestantism resolute, as one can readily see in her lifelong hostility to the revival of Marianism. Waller's observation is very much to the point: '[Rossetti's] spiritual adviser [i.e. William Dodsworth] during her impressionable adolescence [was an] improbable combination of High Church activist and premillenialist preacher that would mold the peculiar configuration of her religious sensibility' (p. 466).

—Jerome J. McGann. "Periodization and Christina Rossetti." *The Beauty of Inflections: Literary Investigations in Historical Method and Theory.* Oxford: Clarendon Press, 1985: 220–229.

CRITICAL ANALYSIS OF
"Remember"

Christina Rossetti's poem "Remember" opens with an injunction, "remember me when I am gone", and that given to a love in the present haunts whatever joy may actually exist. "Remember me" is both a demand for the future, and a looking back from the future towards the past. It contains a prophetic pronouncement that is already an anticipatory nostalgia. As opposed to the fatherly ghost in "Hamlet", who is come back from the "silent land" demanding the rights of memory, Rossetti's speaker asks for something else: "only remember me". This "only" is both command to another and lament for oneself. The speaker asks for a memory that is to "late" for "counsel" or "prayer", and a memory that is not "grief". While forgetfulness is loosely equated with "darkness and corruption", we soon learn that this corruption is a species of memory, and not simply of forgetfulness:

> Yet if you should forget me for a while
> And afterwards remember, do not grieve:
> For if the darkness and corruption leave
> A vestige of the thoughts that once I had,
> Better by far you should forget and smile
> Than that you should remember and be sad.

A temporary forgetfulness followed by a grief riddled and forced remembrance is not what Rossetti intended. Such activity is only partial, a 'vestige of the thoughts that once I had'. In effect, the person asking for memory is put in the position of remembering, because it is that person imagining their own aftermath, imagining their own future remembrance. And so, the call for memory, if imperfect, becomes a call for a pleasant forgetfulness. The speaker suspects their own call for memory, because their call for memory may be 'the thoughts that once I had'. This posture is best glossed by the poems image of the speaker as half turning to go, yet turning to stay. This image is offered by the speaker as a mutual remembrance, but simultaneously as a future possibility. One can almost imagine the temporal speculation of the poem rotating around the speaker, or the speaker rotating within this network.

We begin the poem comfortably assuming that it is a suggestion for a time after the speakers death, an assumption that is belied by the demands the poem contains:

> Remember me when no more day by day
>   You tell me of our future that you planned:
>   Only remember me; you understand
>   It will be late to counsel then or pray.

Read one way, these lines sound like a lamentation. Read another, they sound like "you will only be able to remember me when you stop telling me of the future you have planned for us", with the "you" feeling more than a little accusatory. Then the line "Only remember me" becomes more insistent, and less forgiving. Read in this way, the poem seems to call out for a space of pure memory, free of speculation and planning. "Only" can be read as an impassioned cry and as a restrictive demand. Importantly, while the poem seems to be about an event in the future that will call for memory, it begins to feel more and more like advice for today.

The call to remember assumes that the caller has a perfect idea of their commemoration in mind, and in this way is very demanding. Of course, this call also leaves a lot up to the person who receives it, who, after all, is supposedly the one doing the remembering. In Christina Rossetti's poem "Remember", the progression seems to be: "remember me when I am gone", "we are alive now and the way you plan for the future, by telling me about those plans, will resemble the way I want you to remember when that future is no longer possible", "an imperfect memory of my mind and of my love, caused by a period of forgetfulness, while dark and corrupt, is nothing to grieve about because it is better to forget and smile than it is to remember and be sad".

"Remember"

HAROLD BLOOM ON THE USES OF REMEMBRANCE

[In this excerpt, Professor Bloom describes the five uses of "remember" and how Rossetti employs them in her poem.]

Her "Remember" sonnet is a superb instance of Christina Rossetti's hushed, understated originality. Few anticipated self-elegies speak so adequately to a survivor in the voice of the beloved dead. Christina's subtle art plays upon the five uses of "remember" in her sonnet, all of them very different from one another. The first is simple or literal remembrance, while the second alludes to the potential guilt of the survivor. "Only remember me," the third, is more plangent with regret, while "afterwards remember" is no reproof, since grieving is inappropriate for the respites granted by erotic loss. The final "remember" is the most gracious, gently testifying to the selfless element in the love that is lost.

> —Harold Bloom. "Dante Gabriel Rossetti and Christina Rossetti." *Genius: A Mosaic of One Hundred Exemplary Creative Minds.* Warner Books, 2002: 432.

MARGARET REYNOLDS ON ALTERNATIVE READINGS OF THE POEM

[Margaret Reynolds is a Reader in the School of English and Drama at Queen Mary, University of London. She is well known for her study of Victorian women's poetry, and she has also written on Elizabeth Barrett Browning's *Aurora Leigh*.]

Listen to what she says in 'Remember'.

Remember me when I am gone away,
   Gone far away into the silent land;
   When you can no more hold me by the hand,
Nor I half turn to go yet turning stay.
Remember me when no more day by day
   You tell me of our future that you planned:
   Only remember me; you understand
It will be late to counsel then or pray.
Yet if you should forget me for a while
   And afterwards remember, do not grieve:
   For if the darkness and corruption leave
A vestige of the thoughts that once I had,
Better by far you should forget and smile
   Than that you should remember and be sad. (*CP*, 1:37)

The first question to ask is then: remember ... what? Of course, the answer looks like "me." "Remember me" is repeated three times in the first eight lines and the title of the sonnet is often mistakenly given as "Remember me." But it's a Rossetti trick. As the poem moves on to the sestet the instruction to "remember" appears twice, but in neither case is it made clear exactly what may, or may not, be remembered there. Everyone knows, or feels as if they know, this poem. It's in all the anthologies, it's on all the poetry request programs. It's popular because it's short, neat, and has no difficult words in it (with the possible exception of "vestige"), and perhaps above all, because it seems to embody the romantic ideal of self-sacrificing womanhood that is to be demanded of a poem where the signature at the bottom relentlessly overdetermines interpretation. Rossetti scholars fall into the trap. W. David Shaw says that in this lyric of "barely repressed pain"

> Rossetti discovers that the most exquisite and refined torture is, not to be forgotten by her beloved, but to inflict suffering on him. Tactful concern for the lover now displaces any self-centered desire to live on in his memory.... "Harsh towards herself, towards others full of ruth." That line (5) from "A Portrait" seems to me the best single comment on the courtesy and ease with which the sonnet "Remember" absorbs the pain of death, turning self-regard into an exquisitely refined contest in gentility and tact.

Exquisite, refined, genteel, selfless, tactful; William Michael would have recognized this Christina.

"Remember" looks like a love poem. But then that might mean that we have already made assumptions about who is speaking to whom that go beyond what is actually, in the text. Apart from knowing a woman to be the author, why do we take it that this is a woman speaking? Because, in de Beauvoir's terms, "He is the Subject, he is the Absolute—she is the Other." The (supposed) listener/man in this poem is obviously someone out there in the world doing things, he is "one"; she, the speaker/woman, is clearly "Other"—she doesn't have an independent existence beyond this relationship. She is anxious that he should remember her (and she goes on about it so much that the implication is that he won't), so that she will exist.

The active/passive opposition set out in this poem further implies a feminine signature. Cixous's "Sorties" diagram lines up activity, along with sun, culture, day, father, head, logos, with the masculine principle while the feminine principle lines up with passivity, moon, nature, night, mother, heart, pathos. The ultimate passivity for women, enacted so often in Rossetti's poems, explicit in "After Death" and hinted at in "Remember," is death. Not that there's any reason here to explain why this speaker is about to die. The referent is absent, but presumed, because the condition of (assumed) femininity includes the condition of passivity and death. "The silent land" is pretty vague, and "the darkness and corruption" not much better, but nonetheless the idea that this speaker is about to die is quite acceptable in our cultural positioning; women die, men mourn, it's a classic literary trope and one that Rossetti exploits to the full. Interestingly it's quite hard to turn it the other way around, because then what would a he-speaker be dying of? going to war? There are few possibilities. Men have to die for a reason; women just do.

So. The nice version of this poem goes: "Please remember me when I'm dead, but on the other hand, if it's going to make you unhappy to remember me, then I love you so much ('For if the darkness and corruption leave / A vestige of the thoughts that once I had') that I'd rather that you did forget about me so that you can be happy."

It is true that this reading is in the poem. But it's not the only one. As Angela Leighton has observed, "Behind Rossetti's 'Aesthetic of Renunciation' it is possible to discern an alternative aesthetics of secrecy, self-containment, and caprice." And the clue to the capricious reading lies in the verbs. The first verb to appear is the odd construction applied to the speaker, "when I am gone away." That the verb here is "to be" used in the present tense to convey a future idea, and without any active verb-construction—like "When I have gone away"—applied to the speaker, makes the sentence feel oddly passive. By contrast in the opening octet the listener is given active verbs lining him (it/they/she) up with the masculine principle and making the *listener* the dominant party. "When you can no more hold me by the hand" ... so he does the holding; "I half turn to go yet turning stay" ... so she makes a move away, but doesn't quite manage that bid for independence; when no more day by day / You tell me of our future that you planned" ... *our* future? that you planned? ... so she didn't have a say in it; "It will be late to counsel then or pray." ... O.K., is that what he does all the time? goes on at her, giving advice and asking her to do things?

The way these verbs work means that this speaker manages, almost secretly, subtextually, to reveal that the he-listener is the chief actor in their relationship. In life she, the speaker, is "use-value." He uses her for whatever agenda it is that he has in mind, personal or social, and she has no say in anything. (Except, of course, through the medium of the poem.) He acts and she is acted upon.

Just as he acts and she is acted upon in "After Death." Interestingly, in both poems the same image, the same idea of action, appears. In "Remember" the speaker looks toward the day "When you can no more hold me by the hand." In "After Death" the he-presence in the poem does not "take my hand in his." It's a resonant absence—or presence. The father takes the child by the hand; the father lover takes the beloved by the hand; patriarchy takes a hand and she is taken, wherever this père-verted discourse is organized.

What about the pretty end then?—"if the darkness and corruption leave / A vestige of the thoughts that, once I had."

What thoughts are these? Thus far, they all seem to be cross, fed-up thoughts about how he is bullying her and lecturing her. Maybe then *these* are the thoughts that will get left behind, the traces, like fossils left on the face of the earth. And maybe the "darkness and corruption" here is not death (as in the nice version), but the darkness and corruption of her anger, her distress, at his conventional use of her. No wonder then that he should "forget and smile" because, maybe, just maybe, what is going on here is not that she wants him to forget so that he can be happy because she loves him so much, but that if he remembers, and remembers the truth, then he will be sad. And the implication is that so he should be, because he's going to realize what a shit he's been all along. "Better by far" does not sound much like a generous valedictory wish any more; it sounds like a curse, a threat, a bitter promise that is perverse and "sweet" and cruel in the mouth of the vengeful speaker.

Once upon a time Christina Rossetti was simple.

But Christina loved games, puns, parodies, and secrets, and while William Michael and so many later readers have mooned over the "broken-hearted"-ness of her poetry, Rossetti has played a joke. Self-effacing, hidden, secret, behind, underneath, are words that are often associated with Rossetti, yet what goes on in that underneath, still needs excavation. The curiously throwaway reference to an evolutionary context that appears in "Remember" may provide a model. "Darkness and corruption" may, after all, be the troubled present, the nineteenth century itself, the period of Rossetti's own lived life, fraught with personal and social prohibitions that make indirect speaking necessary. But still in that place a trace may be left of the individual life, a vestige of (self) creation. Others coming after, remembering Rossetti, will be able to read the trace of the hidden life beneath the cover story. Not that the one excludes the other. "After Death" and "Remember" both have (at least) two readings. In each case a subversive text is inscribed within a complaisant poem, but they are simultaneously compatible.

In 1856 Christina Rossetti wrote a story about a picture called "The Lost Titian." It was published in, *The Crayon* in New York and was later included in Rossetti's *Commonplace and Other Short*

Stories (1870). Dante Gabriel called this collection "the most everyday affair possible" but he misses the point. Compiling the commonplace book, a scrapbook or family album containing favorite quotations, recipes, autographs, and illustrations, provided a familiar domestic occupation for Victorian women; and scrapbooks, with all their implications for doubleness, text and revised text, fragments reworked, were a preoccupation with his sister. There is also a curious echo here in the title, which Christina said she just couldn't manage to improve. Years since, when Dante Gabriel had shown John Ruskin Christina's *Goblin Market*, Ruskin had declared

> no publisher—I am deeply grieved to know this—would take them, so full are they of quaintness and other offences. Irregular measure ... is the calamity of modern poetry.... Your sister should exercise herself in the severest commonplace of metre until she can write as the public like.

Doubtless Dante Gabriel showed the letter to Christina; doubtless the remembered it; doubtless she replied with her title. Another Christina pun, another joke, another hidden text.

"The Lost Titian" tells the story of Gianni, a colleague and rival of Titian's in Renaissance Venice. Gianni is a successful and popular painter, but his life and his methods are suspect, and his position is threatened by Titian's preeminence, soon to be confirmed by the unveiling of his latest masterpiece. One night, in an apparently friendly game of dice, Titian, drunk with wine and success, stakes his newly created work—and Gianni wins. Jealous of the Master's fame, Gianni daubs over the picture with coarse pigments, and then, on the blank surface, he paints "a dragon flaming, clawed, preposterous." Falling from favor and into debt, Gianni is beset by his creditors, who are unaware of the presence of Titian's masterpiece, while Titian himself does not recognize his own painting. To Gianni's horror, the dragon is nonetheless claimed by another creditor who takes a fancy to its gaudy show and sets it up as an inn sign. Gianni spends the rest of his life trying to paint a new dragon that will be accepted in satisfactory exchange, but to no avail. So when Gianni dies, still silent, Titian's masterpiece remains hidden, lost forever. Or "perhaps not quite lost": "Reader, should you chance to discern over wayside inn or metropolitan hotel a dragon pendent, or should you find such an effigy amid the lumber of a broker's shop, whether it be red, green or piebald, demand it importunately, pay for it liberally, and in the privacy of home scrub it. It may be that from behind the dragon will emerge a fair one, fairer than Andromeda, and that to you will appertain the honor of yet further exalting Titian's greatness in the eyes of a world."

The double texts of Rossetti's poems are the other way round, of course. Underneath the "fair one" with her smooth surface is a "preposterous" dragon who nonetheless is an Andromeda waiting to be unchained. And when that cruel-perverse-Rossetti-dragon is revealed, it will contribute to Rossetti's greatness: "Reader ... in the privacy of home scrub it." In the privacy of "home" the "unheimlich" will be uncovered. "Uncanny" is a word often associated with Rossetti's poetry and it's a right word. As a good Victorian daughter and sister Rossetti is always at home—"almost constantly in the same house." And yet her poetry is "unheimlich" because it speaks, and it says more than it means. Rossetti wrote in secret and she wrote secrets. Not necessarily her own, but everybody's secrets. Her poetry is our talking-cure. Her protagonists speak, confess, tell. In their nightmares and their dreams they compulsively repeat the traumas of desire and loss. Her dead women are the corpses who have fallen (cadaver/cadere) and lost themselves in decay, but they paradoxically project (abject/throw out/throw up) a hidden self, a vital self, in the process. Squeezed in between, or out between, the spaces in the text is the secret message, written "in white ink" that seeps and oozes through the page. In Kristeva's terms, the semiotic speaks through, or beyond, or out of, the symbolic. The symbolic in Rossetti is always that "excessively neat" surface held together by the decorum of the "single guarantee: syntax." But "underlying the written," and quite as meaningful, even more powerful, is the silent speaking space, "enigmatic and feminine ... rhythmic, unfettered, irreducible to its intelligible verbal translation ... musical, anterior to judgement." But you have to listen hard. At the center of both

"After Death" and "Remember" there is a silence. In "After Death" there "Came a deep silence" just before the speaker lets out the second bitter text. In "Remember" the speaker projects herself into a time when she will be gone away "into the silent land" and her second bitter text might be remembered. But it has, mostly, been forgotten, or rather, not heard. In the double texts of Rossetti's poems her "two lips" may speak together but they may also mumble into silence.

—Margaret Reynolds. "Speaking Unlikenesses." *Textual Practice*, January 1997: 12–17.

"A Birthday"

In this poem, the "birthday of my life" and the arrival of a lover are said to be more or less equivalent, although the final couplet does admit some ambiguity: "Because the birthday of my life / is come, my love is come to me" could be read either "because the birthday of my life has happened, now my love is come to me", or "the birthday of my life has finally come because my love is come to me". Read the first way, the birthday of the poet's life causes the arrival of the lover; read the second, the coming of the lover precipitates the birthday. The events seem codependent, and either way the marking of the passage of time is curiously mixed with the prospect of love, a love that seems to have been anticipated. The difference depends on whether the emotion inspired by the birthday of one's life and the coming of a lover are the same, or how similar we take the events to be. The two happenings are compared, and the poem seems aware of its own use of comparison. Ultimately, the claim is that the poet's heart is "gladder" than the sum of its imagery. The monumentalizing function of the poem's imagery is both enlarged and reduced by the explicitly repetitive use of comparison, an event the formality of which is itself like the inevitably exciting redundancy of a birthday.

Temporally, the cyclical nature of one's birthday is compared with the potential singular, unique arrival of a lover. Both things are affected by the comparison. The repetitiveness of the celebration of a birthday feels more like the birthday, and the uniqueness of the lover's arrival is diffused throughout the sum of a lifetime of birthday celebrations, mixing hope and gratitude. When we finish the poem, we realize that "the birthday of my life" does not necessarily refer to the poet's birthday at all, and that she could be using it metaphorically to refer to any happening that inspires a gladness that must be temporarily understood.

In the first stanza, a series of similes are introduced, simply in the first line of each couples with a slight modification in the second. In each couplet, the first half sets up equivalence between the poet's heart and an object: "My heart is like a singing bird", "My heart is like an apple tree", and "My heart is like a rainbow shell". The second half of each couplet alters the radiant purity of each image, in a not so straightforward way. The "singing bird" is in a "watered shoot", and so our sense of its freedom is somewhat altered. The boughs of the apple tree are "bent with thickset fruit", an image of potential and fecundity, but again of a kind of restraint, or restriction that is at its limit case. In each case, the modification of the image produces an excess, in order to support the final claim that the poet's heart is "gladder than all these".

Christina Rossetti was often mocked in print for the exuberance displayed by the poem, and she herself said that she could "not account" for the joy it evoked. The images in the poem have an emblematic history. The word "halcyon" means calm, and is taken from a bird in an ancient fable thought to breed during the winter solstice on a nest floating in the sea. The nest charmed the wind and waves, and it was thought that the sea was especially calm during this period. "Vair" is a fur obtained from squirrels of black and white coloration, and is a frequent part of heraldic ballads. The "fleur-de-lys" is the heraldic lily that is emblazoned on the royal arms of France.

"A Birthday"

HAROLD BLOOM ON DANTE GABRIEL AND CHRISTINA'S INFLUENCE ON EACH OTHER

[In this excerpt, Professor Bloom demonstrates how Dante Gabriel Rossetti and Christina Rossetti "illuminated" each other's creativity and work.]

Her touch is invariably very light, her voice pitched low, but disturbingly felt. And, though very rarely, she can be ecstatic and celebratory, and we gladly help her celebrate "A Birthday":

My heart is like a singing bird
　　Whose nest is in a watered shoot:
My heart is like an apple-tree
　　Whose boughs are bent with thickset fruit;
My heart is like a rainbow shell
　　That paddles in a halcyon sea;
My heart is gladder than all these
　　Because my love is come to me.

Raise me a dais of silk and down;
　　Hang it with vair and purple dyes;
Carve it in doves and pomegranates,
　　And peacocks with a hundred eyes;
Work it in gold and silver grapes,
　　In leaves and silver fleur-de-lys;
Because the birthday of my life
　　Is come, my love is come to me.　　(...)

Christina Rossetti, a poet of genius by any standards, remains in many ways an enigma. An Anglo-Catholic devotional writer, original and in some regards esoteric, she does not assimilate easily to the methods and aims of what now regards itself as feminist literary criticism, and which finds in her "the aesthetics of renunciation." The poetry of renunciation in fact need not be either religious or feminine: its major exemplar was the pagan Goethe. A pagan closer up was Christina's remarkable older brother, the poet-painter Dante Gabriel Rossetti, whose intense erotomania provided ample provocation to his sister's ultimate rejection of what our culture still exalts as "romantic love."

Dante Gabriel Rossetti's painting may be regarded as a question of taste; his poetry now enjoys less critical reputation than his sister's, but time will alter that, since the power of his best work transcends fashion, whereas the paintings, for the larger part, may indeed be period pieces. I bring brother and sister together here because they illuminate each other, and the family resemblances (and differences) of genius have their own value and fascination. Elsewhere in this book I juxtapose the James brothers, and two of the Brontë sisters, but neither of these comparisons seem to me so potentially fecund as reading, side by side, the erotic poems of Dante Gabriel Rossetti and the poems of his sister, in their own way sometimes erotic, but always with a difference.

Despite some surface impressions, both Rossettis are difficult poets. Close reading nowadays becomes more problematic: there are few who want to (or can) teach it, and a visually oriented generation is reluctant to learn. Christina (I will use first names so as to stop repeating "Rossetti") is at her strongest when she dissolves all differences between poetry sacred and secular:

Passing away, saith the World, passing away:
Chances, beauty, and youth, sapped day by day:
Thy life never continueth in one stay.
Is the eye waxen dim, is the dark hair changing to grey
That hath won neither laurel nor bay?
I shall clothe myself in Spring and bud in May:
Thou, root-stricken, shalt not rebuild thy decay
On my bosom for aye.
Then I answered: Yea.

Passing away, saith my Soul, passing away:
With its burden of fear and hope, of labour and play,
Hearken what the past doth witness and say:
Rust in thy gold, a moth is in thine array,

A canker is in thy bud, thy leaf must decay.
A midnight, at cockcrow, at morning, one certain day
Lo the Bridegroom shall come and shall not delay;
Watch thou and pray.
Then I answered: Yea.

Passing away, saith my God, passing away:
Winter passeth after the long delay:
New grapes on the vine, new figs on the tender spray,
Turtle calleth turtle in Heaven's May.
Though I tarry, wait for Me, trust Me, watch and pray:
Arise, come away, night is past and to it is day,
My love, My sister, My spouse, thou shalt hear Me say.
Then I answered: Yea.

This was printed as the third of "Old and New Year Ditties," but it far surpasses the first two. One hesitates to call Christina a mystic, another John of the Cross or Teresa, because her obsessive emphasis, like Dante Gabriel's, lingers always on the Inferno of sexual love. Despite her biographers, she has largely kept her secrets. We know little about her "love life," an oxymoron for most people, and particularly for her older brother. She declined at least two marriage proposals, supposedly from religious scruples, but I suspect her pride and independence determined her single status, her vision of herself as a writer.

—Harold Bloom "Dante Gabriel Rossetti and Christina Rossetti." *Genius: A Mosaic of One Hundred Exemplary Creative Minds.* Warner Books, 2002: 432–434.

LYNDA PALAZZO ON THE MEANS OF REPRESENTATION

[Lynda Palazzo teaches at The King's School in Macclesfield in the United Kingdom. She has recently published *Christina Rossetti's Feminist Theology*.]

I would like to suggest that the difficulties in interpreting such poems as 'A Birthday' stem from a tacit agreement among the majority of critics that the study of Christina Rossetti's poetry does not involve a study of the development in poetic thought of the time. Was she, as Festa tells us, concerned exclusively with 'the retelling of the truths which she found in her religion'?[6] To limit her poetry in this way is to ignore any theoretical background to her composition. Yet there are very definite indications that Rossetti was familiar with contemporary poetic theory. W.D. Shaw's study of her poem 'Good Friday' is one demonstration of the direct or indirect influence on her of the poetic theory of E.S. Dallas.[7]

If we allow a similar theoretical basis for a poem such as 'A Birthday', the elements of the poem immediately fall into place and Rossetti can be seen experimenting with aesthetic ideas which resemble those of her brother Dante Gabriel. Take for example a passage from Dallas' *Poetics: An Essay on Poetry*:

> *And every pleasure too, has a degree of its own at which it becomes poetry, just as ice, glass and iron have each a degree at which they melt ... so certain moods of the mind, such as love and feeling generally, contain so much imagination as to be almost always poetic.*[8]

Here Dallas implies that the stronger, more intense an emotion, the more it is poetic. Why not then view 'A Birthday' as an experiment in the *representation* of an intensely 'poetic' sensation, that of 'Love's ecstatic gratification.'[9] It is the *means* of representation which is being examined by Rossetti.

Let us examine the images of the first stanza. They are not only figures 'recalled in their natural element'[10] but are each representations of a moment of fulfilment in a sense both sensual and sexual. The 'singing bird' (2.1) has found a mate and expresses his joy in song—as the poet wishes to express hers. The apple tree is representative of another time of fulfilment in nature, as is the shell which simply suggests the highest expression of fulfilment which nature has to offer in its hint of the birth of Aphrodite.

All these images seem to be very effective. Why then are they insufficient to portray the emotion felt? Why is the speaker's heart 'gladder than all these' (2.7)? It is because the images are manifestations found in nature and therefore subject to time and decay. Festa agrees with Lynde's observation that the figures in the second stanza are superior to those in the first because they have been 'reworked by a creative art.'[11] However, far more important in our examination of the poem is the consideration of the second stanza as a complete image in itself, the human response to the intensity of the emotion felt. In an attempt to immortalise such an emotion, mankind responds with an act of artistic creation, and here we remember Lynde's observation that Rossetti was the sister of a painter and that the objects of the second stanza are not only popular ones in Victorian representational art but are also those to be found particularly in the paintings of Dante Gabriel Rossetti, framing the central figure which was usually a woman.

The second stanza, then, is remarkably similar to the background of a Pre-Raphaelite painting. But where is the central figure? The words 'Raise me a dais' (1.9) may mean not only the instruction of a craftsman to his assistants but may also mean 'Raise in our honour, a dais'. In other words, the speaker of the poem (a woman like Rossetti herself) would then take her place on the dais. Rossetti certainly had ample experience of posing as the central figure for such canvases. Thus she has chosen as the highest representation of an intense human emotion the Pre-Raphaelite painting, and it may be seen that the poem outlines a similar aesthetic to that which Dante Gabriel proposes in 'Hand and Soul' where the fixed image of a female figure was used to convey the artistic message.

Yet the choice of detail in the second stanza shows an awareness, typical of Rossetti, of the Christian implication of such an aesthetic. The similarity in tone and diction of the second stanza to the raising of the tabernacle recorded in *Exodus*[12] shows us that she recognized this artistic process as the raising of a temple—not to God, but to the beauty of a human emotion.

Here we may briefly refer to a poem which Rossetti composed ten days before 'A Birthday', 'Memory I.'[13] The speaker in this poem describes a bitter choice made in the breaking down of an idol which had been set up in her heart:

None know the choice I made and broke my heart,
Breaking my idol: I have braced my will
Once, chosen for once my part.

(ll. 14–16)

L.M. Packer quotes in this connection a passage from Rossetti's prose work, *Letter and Spirit*:

The idolater substitutes in his heart and worship something material in lieu of God; and as being material, akin to himself and unlike God ...[14]

If Rossetti were concerned about the breaking down of idols, in the composition of 'Memory I', it is quite possible that she was still similarly concerned in the writing of 'A Birthday'.

NOTES

6. Festa, p. 50.
7. 'Projection and Empathy in Victorian Poetry.' *VP* 19:4 (1981) pp. 315–336.
8. E.S. Dallas, *Poetics: An Essay on Poetry*, London, 1852; rpt., New York: Johnson Reprint Corporation, 1969. p. 47.
9. Packer, p. 115.
10. Festa, p. 52.
11. *Ibid.*
12. ... thou shalt make the tabernacle with ten curtains; of fine turned linen, and blue and purple, and scarlet, with cherubim the work of the cunning workmen shalt thou make them.
Exodus 26.1
13. Crump, p. 147. Composed Nov. 8 1857.
14. Packer, p. 114.

—Lynda Palazzo. "Notes & Reviews: Christina Rossetti's 'A Birthday': Representations of the 'Poetic'". *The Journal of Pre-Raphaelite Studies* vol. VII, no. 2, May 1987: 94–95.

RICHARD D. LYNDE ON THE NATURAL WORLD
AND IMAGERY

[Richard D. Lynde has published "A Note on the Imagery in Christina Rossetti's 'A Birthday'" in *Victorian Poetry*.]

Whatever the reasons for its existence, an examination of the natural and artificially made objects which it embodies will provide a fascinating glimpse into the associative method of the mind which produced it. The three natural objects of the first stanza, the singing bird, the apple tree, and the rainbow shell, appear in their native settings. As Christina herself said: "Common things continually at hand, wind or windfall or budding bough, acquire a sacred association, and cross our path under aspects at once familiar and transfigured."[3] The objects found in the second stanza, the doves and pomegranates, the peacocks, the gold and silver grapes, and the leaves and silver fleurs-de-lys, either do not appear in their natural settings or else are artistic renderings of natural objects. They are commanded by the speaker of the poem to be wrought in likeness upon a dais. The pomegranates are a particularization of the fruit of the apple tree in stanza one, while the doves and peacocks may be related to the bird in that stanza. All the images in the second half of the poem, however, traditionally bear religious meaning—even though their meaning here is secular—and reflect an awareness of traditional Christian art.

Besides Christina Rossetti's direct familiarity with the natural world as it is represented in the first stanza, and her knowledge of religious symbols as it appears in the second, there remain two less obvious sources which may have suggested some of the imagery in the poem. The first is in the world of commonplace Victorian representational art. The pomegranate, for example, occupied a prominent position in Georgian architecture, where it figured in fruit and flower mouldings. And the peacock was, in mid-nineteenth-century England, commonly depicted as a modern Indian symbol woven into fabrics imported from that country. Another connection between the commercial world and the poem is suggested by the tradesmen's signs still found in some places in England, particularly the cities. In the second stanza of "A Birthday" the speaker gives commands to craftsmen who are obviously dyers: "Raise me a dais of silk and down; / Hang it with vair and purple dyes." As the painted sign of the dyer in England traditionally included the peacock, the rainbow, and the dove together, and as all of these appear in the short space of the poem, quite possibly the author's observation of such a sign suggested this otherwise random combination.

A final possible source of imagery in this lyric is a unique one connected with Christina Rossetti's personal history. She was the sister of an artist. "Her older brother was an art critic; her first lover was an artist; she drew designs and illustrations for some of her own poems. It came naturally to her to regard everything as the possible foundation of a picture."[4] And she had even posed for some of her brother's paintings. In 1848–50 he had been working on an Annunciation (*Ecce Ancilla Domini*) for which Christina had modelled the Virgin. On this canvas the Angel is holding a prominent lily which greatly resembles a series of fleurs-de-lys, while another lily is depicted upon a sampler which the Virgin had been embroidering. A dove represents the Holy Spirit, as is traditional. In another of her brother's religious works, an oil entitled *The Girlhood of Mary Virgin*, started also in 1848 and for which she sat, appear a dove, a lily, and grape bunches. These pictorial images from both paintings appear little more than a decade later in "A Birthday."

Their presence in the poem is consistent with William Michael Rossetti's observation that Christina's "habits of composing were eminently of the spontaneous kind ... something impelled her feelings, or 'came into her head,' and her hand obeyed the dictation."[5] The freely associative method within which Christina worked probably led her to interrelate in this poem diverse images remembered from direct observation, from traditional Christian myth and artistic religious symbolism, from acquaintance with commercial art of her day, and finally from her unique experiences and memories as a member of an artistic family.

NOTES

3. *Seek and Find* (London, 1879), p. 14.

4 Marjory A. Bald, "Christina Rossetti," *Women-Writers of the Nineteenth Century* (London, 1923), p. 253.

5. In his Preface to *New Poems by Christina Rossetti* (London, 1896), p. xiii.

—Richard D. Lynde. "A Note on the Imagery in Christina Rossetti's 'A Birthday'". *Victorian Poetry* vol. III, no. 4, autumn 1965: 261–263.

JAMES F. DOUBLEDAY ON THE JUXTAPOSITION OF
IMAGES

[James F. Doubleday has published "Rossetti's A Birthday"
in *The Explicator*.]

The effect of "A Birthday" comes in part from the tension
between two very different kinds of images and two very
different means by which these images are expressed. In the first
stanza, the means is a series of similes—the simplest and most
"natural" means of conveying an image. And the images
themselves are all natural ones: The singing bird, the thick-
laden apple-tree, the rainbow shell. But these images are in an
order of increasing distance. We can easily empathize with a
singing bird. It is more difficult to feel with a tree. And when we
come to the shell, particularly a shell that is given life (it
"paddles") and placed in a "halcyon" sea, in a world of mythic
peace and tranquility, we have an image that is very hard to
realize imaginatively. Even so, the speaker finally rejects all three
natural images as inadequate to represent the splendor of her
feeling: "My heart is gladder than all these."
 So the next stanza uses a far different means and far different
images. The speaker, like an empress, commands the
construction of a dais to her specifications. The images are rich,
strange, exotic, Eastern: silk and down, vair and purple dyes,
pomegranates and peacocks, gold and silver work. But these
images are likewise inadequate to represent the speaker's
experience. Therefore, after images from nature and art, the final
image, the "birthday," is from common human life. But it is life
raised to a higher power: "the birthday of my life," the beginning
of the *vita nuova*.

—James F. Doubleday. "Rossetti's A Birthday". From *The
Explicator* vol. 44, no. 2, winter 1986: 29–30.

CRITICAL ANALYSIS OF

"Up-Hill"

This poem begins with what could be a simple question, and gives a seemingly straightforward answer to that question. As we progress through the poem, however, we realize that the question is more figurative than literal, and the journey that the poem describes is the inevitable human one towards death. By describing death as an Inn, however, the poet suggests that, after a night of rest, the journey may continue. The inn is all inclusive, in that there are "beds for all who come". The quality of one's rest in the inn is nonetheless subject to some higher interpretation, as it is a direct function, or "sum", of the labour one has performed over the course of a lifetime.

The difference, in the poem, between day and night has to do with the speed and quality of time. The day's journey, or life as we know it, is long and takes "from morn to night". Once rest begins, after the setting of the sun, the hours become "slow and dark", although not imperceptible. In general, the sense of sight in the poem is subjected to the poem's temporality, so that the spiritual progress it enacts overwhelms our common sense of space and time. The form of the poem, that of a seemingly clear and somewhat rhetorical question that furnishes us with a somewhat tenebrous rhetorical answer, is crucial to Rossetti's poetry, and biblical in feel.

CRITICAL VIEWS ON
"Up-Hill"

HAROLD BLOOM ON THE MEANING OF THE POEM

[In this excerpt, Professor Bloom explains his interpretation
of Rossetti's poem, "Up-Hill."]

It is very peculiar that both Rossettis now strike many unthinking
readers as rather tame, since both sister and brother frighten me
as poets, the more I ponder them. Christina would not yield to
Dante Gabriel's self-destructiveness: the quality of her Christian
faith, severely intellectualized, saved her. And yet it is not an easy
faith to comprehend, whatever your own beliefs or skepticisms.
Here is her extraordinary "Up-Hill," a poem I loved, but
misunderstood, for many years:

> Does the road wind up-hill all the way?
> Yes, to the very end.
> Will the day's journey take the whole long day?
> From morn to night, my friend.
>
> But is there for the night a resting-place?
> A roof for when the slow dark hours begin.
> May not the darkness hide it from my face?
> You cannot miss that inn.
>
> Shall I meet other wayfarers at night?
> Those who have gone before.
> Then must I knock, or call when just in sight?
> They will not keep you standing at that door.
>
> Shall I find comfort, travel-sore and weak?
> Of labour you shall find the sum.
> Will there be beds for me and all who seek?
> Yea, beds for all who come.

Jerome McGann first noted the apparent oddness of these two
final lines, which can seem a grotesque parody of Christian hope,

until you realize—as he shows—that Christina adheres to the strange Adventist doctrine of "Soul Sleep." What happens to the Christian's soul between the moment of her death and the Great Advent of Christ's Second Coming? Does the soul go directly to a Last Judgment, and then wait patiently in Paradise for a Resurrected Body to join it? Or does it sleep a long sleep until at Millennium it wakes up forever? Christina firmly adhered to the latter view, a conviction that governs not only "Up-Hill," but a considerable number of her more interesting poems.

I depart (with gratitude) from McGann's deeply informed historicism to surmise that "Soul Sleep" allowed Christina to hope that her charismatic but self-destructive older brother would yet escape his erotic inferno in the vast slumber before his own resurrection. Her final devotional book, *The Face of the Deep* (1892), is the least judgmental commentary upon the Apocalypse of Saint John the Divine that I have ever read. I give the last word here to her charming memoir "The House of Dante Gabriel Rossetti," also published in 1892, two years before her own death. She recalls the marvelous assemblage of friends and creatures who surrounded her brother in his home on Cheyne Walk in London, ranging from Algernon Swinburne and George Meredith to an owl named Bobby and a wombat called McGregor, and beholds them all as a vision by Lewis Carroll:

> With such inhabitants, Tudor House and its grounds became a sort of wonderland, and once the author of *Wonderland* photographed us in the garden.

It is a comfort to think back to that moment, in the autumn of 1863, when the Reverend Charles Dodgson photographed the Rossettis and the menagerie in Dante Gabriel's garden. After so much erotic travail, one wants to think of Alice, and the Snark.

—Harold Bloom. "Dante Gabriel Rossetti and Christina Rossetti." Genius: A Mosaic of One Hundred Exemplary Creative Minds. Warner Books, 2002: 432–434.

EUGENE J. BRZENK ON THE LINKS BETWEEN
"UP-HILL" AND "AMOR MUNDI"

[Eugene J. Brzenk has published "Up-Hill and Down" in
Victorian Poetry. He also edited *Imaginary Portraits* by Walter
Pater.]

I wish to make a detailed, side-by-side examination of these two
poems ["Amor Mundi" and "Up-Hill"] to show that they are
more closely linked than Mrs. Packer or other commentators
have indicated, that to read either poem by itself, in fact, is to
miss an entire dimension of meaning and poetic effect. Such an
examination, by giving detailed attention to "Amor Mundi" as
well as to "Up-Hill," will also help to adjust the balance of
critical attention between the two.

The most obvious link between the two poems under
consideration is their central metaphor representing life as a road
or path. Each poem describes one of the ways offered to the
individual in his journey through life; together they present a
pair of contrasting though complementary images which are
truly archetypal, for these divergent roads are found in the
earliest literatures and in all cultures and received definitive
expression in Matthew 7.13–14:

> Enter ye in at the strait gate: for wide is the gate, and broad is the
> way, that leadeth to destruction, and many there be which go in
> thereat:
>
> Because strait is the gate, and narrow is the way, which leadeth
> unto life, and few there be that find it.

There are several other works known to Christina Rossetti from
childhood reading which figure in the background of this pair of
poems. The landscapes of "Amor Mundi" and "Up-Hill," for
example, invite the same kind of allegorical interpretation that is

suggested by such landmarks in Bunyan's *Pilgrim's Progress* as the Strait Way, the Gate, the Hill Difficulty, the Byway to Hell and By-Path Meadow, landmarks which themselves echo the New Testament passage. Two other well-known literary passages using this image of the two roads leading to good and evil, to salvation and damnation, include Spenser's description in Book I of *The Faerie Queene* of the paths leading to the House of Pride ("A broad highway," Canto iv, 17) and the House of Holiness ("For streight and narrow was the way," Canto x, 45) and Ophelia's speech to Laertes in *Hamlet*:

> But, good my brother,
> Do not, as some ungracious pastors do,
> Show me the steep and thorny way to heaven,
> Whiles, like a puffed and reckless libertine,
> Himself the primrose path of dalliance treads
> And recks not his own rede.   (I, iii, 49–54)

Christina Rossetti's use of a paired archetypal image which echoes well-known works of literature not only links "Amor Mundi" and "Up-hill," it accounts for their great concentration of meaning despite their relative brevity.

Examination of other ways in which "Up-Hill" and "Amor Mundi" are linked reveals in both the happy correspondence between form and content. In "Up-Hill," the halting movement of the short lines made up largely of monosyllables reproduces the effort needed to reach "that inn"; there is no increment from each paired question and answer or from stanza to stanza so that each exchange has a finality of its own and further emphasizes the laborious quality of the journey which the poem describes. In "Amor Mundi" the tripping rhythm achieved through the use of anapests and feminine and internal rhymes conveys the ease with which the downhill path is negotiated. The movement of this poem is incremental as realization of the nature of the trip grows in each succeeding stanza until the final climactic reply is given: "'This downhill path is easy, but there's no turning back'." The slowing down at the end of the line is just one more example of the poet's use of rhythm and movement to underscore meanings.

But the relationship of meter and rhythm to mood and theme

in both poems is more than one of exact correspondences. The changing, shifting meter of "Amor Mundi" actually characterizes the primrose-path mentality, but the blithe movement of the poem, recalling nursery rhymes or some of the livelier poems from *Sing-Song*, is ironic since the downhill path is ultimately revealed as "hell's own track." Ironically also, the goal of "Up-Hill" hardly seems inviting with its promise that "Of labour you shall find the sum," yet anyone familiar with Christina Rossetti's personal conception of salvation and the difficult road which leads to it recognizes that the whole movement of the poem is intended to convey this very austere conception. This attention in both poems to movement and rhythm to underline meanings and to characterize contrasting points of view provides another link between them.

The very appearance of each poem on the page indicates something of its nature. The short line lengths of "Up-Hill" give the terse questions and answers of that poem, fittingly, the appearance as well as the sound of a catechism. "Amor Mundi" is, on the other hand, typographically expansive, for the fines of the poem take up the width of a page in collections where most other poems are printed in double columns. It should be noted, however, that cutting the four lines of each stanza exactly in half converts the internal rhymes into end rhymes and produces a poem consisting of five eight-line stanzas rhyming *aaabccxb*. This pattern is repeated with complete regularity in the four remaining stanzas so that the poem could be considered as one made up of the trimeter line which is basic to some of Christina's best known poems. However, the fact that the poet chose to disguise this complex rhyming pattern by making each stanza consist of four long lines with frequent run-ons indicates that it was their sweep and rapidity which she wished to emphasize.

The diction of "Up-Hill" and "Amor Mundi" has the simplicity and directness of folk literature, although the latter draws more heavily than its companion piece upon the stock phrases of such works. It includes the number seven so indispensable to folk rhymers and such archaic-sounding expressions as "lovelocks" "an' it please ye," "doat on," "scaled and hooded worm," "the eternal term" and "thou beatest," but they are scattered throughout the five stanzas so that the poem is not primarily dependent upon them for its effect; the rest of the poem is conventional in its diction, often colloquial, and like "Up-hill," basically Anglo-Saxon. The vocabulary of "Up-Hill," in fact, consists mainly of such familiar nouns as "road," "roof," "inn," "night," "door," "labour," and "beds" and verbs like "take," "begin," "hide," "miss," "meet," "knock," and "find." In both poems it is evident that Christina did not follow her brother Dante Gabriel's practice of reading through old romances for what he called "stunning words for poetry," and the fact that she changed line 18 of "Amor Mundi" which originally read: "This way whereof thou weetest, I fear is hell's own track," indicates clearly that the self-consciously antique was not the effect she wanted.

"Amor Mundi" and "Up-Hill" have other similarities to folk literature in addition to those already mentioned. For example, "Amor Mundi," which Dante Gabriel and Christina Rossetti thought reminiscent of "The Demon Lover," uses question-and-answer dialogue and the journey motif as does the traditional work, and both deal with the theme of temptation, one which is central to many of Christina's poems. Unlike the folk ballad's rather circumstantial account, the Rossetti poem is not primarily concerned with telling a story, and only the second stanza of this literary ballad is essentially narrative. As in "Up-Hill," the basic situation is universalized rather than particularized, and the primary focus in both is psychological, or one might say, existential.

Another characteristic of a large body of folk ballads, the interweaving of the natural and the supernatural, can also be seen in "Up-Hill" and "Amor Mundi," for although the speakers in the two poems are not identified, the second speaker in each, the one who makes reply, seems to be one of "Those who have gone before." Christina Rossetti used the motif of the revenant in a variety of ways in numerous poems; her early sonnet, "After Death," depicts a dead woman speaking as her lover leans over her bier, and in "A Chilly Night," the speaker echoes a refrain often found in traditional ballads as she begs the spirit of her dead mother, "Oh, Mother, make a lonely bed for me." Often the revenants are recriminatory, either because, as in "The Ghost's Petition," excessive mourning has made it impossible for the dead to rest, or because a loved one has broken a vow as in "The Poor Ghost" and "The Hour and the Ghost."

There are many questions concerning the speakers in the two poems (is it significant, for instance, that "Amor Mundi" uses quotation marks to indicate the change of speakers while "Uphill" does not?), and identification of the second speakers as revenants need not be insisted upon although such an interpretation lends depth to this pair of poems and further links them.

The poems' central image also relates them to one other folk ballad dealing with the supernatural, the well-known "Thomas Rymer," in which at one point the Queen of Elfland bids Thomas to lean his head upon her knee as she shows him "fairlies three":

'O see not ye yon narrow road,
    So thick beset wi thorns and briers?
That is the path of righteousness,
    Tho after it but few enquires.

'And see not ye that braid braid road
    That lies across yon lillie leven?
That is the path of wickedness,
    Tho some call it the road to heaven.

'And see not ye that bonny road
    That winds about the fernie brae?
That is the road to fair Elfland,
    Whe[re] thou and I this night maun gae.'
                                                            (Child 37A)

Here the image of the divergent roads open to the individual depicts a third alternative, and it is tempting to speculate whether the poet might eventually have enlarged her pair of poems into the usual triad. But there is little evidence that the bonny road, the one taken by the poet-seer, would have appealed to her, for poems celebrating dedication to art, poetry, and the life of the imagination are conspicuously absent from Christina Rossetti's poetry. "Up-Hill" and "Amor Mundi," in fact, epitomize the contrasting themes of duty and temptation, the two main roads which provide the tension and substance of many of her major works. They might easily have been entitled "Amor Mundi" and "De Contemptu Mundi" or "Down-Hill" and "Up-Hill."

Seeing the two poems side by side has revealed how closely linked they are in subject matter, imagery, theme, form, and language, with folk and ballad themes and motifs as another pervasive link. Most importantly, this reading of the poems has demonstrated that they should be printed as companion pieces, for like the paired poems of Blake's *Songs of Innocence* and *Songs of Experience*, they set off and reinforce one another through their resemblances and contrasts. Hopefully, this study has also shown that "Amor Mundi" is as worthy of critical attention as its more frequently anthologized companion.

—Eugene J. Brzenk. "Up-Hill and Down-". *Victorian Poetry* vol. 10, no. 4, winter 1972: 367–371.

EUGENE ZASADINSKI ON RELIGIOUS INTERPRETATION AND SYMBOLISM

[Eugene Zasadinski has published "Christina Rossetti's 'A Better Resurrection' and 'Up-Hill' Self-Reliance and its Limitations" in *The Journal of Pre-Raphaelite Studies*.]

"Up-Hill" also lends itself easily to conventional Anglican interpretation. The central metaphor states that life is a journey, and the poem is structured as a dialogue between the persona, who asks questions pertaining to the afterlife, and an unknown voice, which replies somewhat enigmatically. Barbara Fass ("Christina Rossetti and St. Agnes' Eve," *VP*, 14, 1976) says (45): "In 'Up-Hill' ... the poet ... prepares to climb ... asking anxiously, however, about what she can expect on her trip." Ralph Bellas (*Christina Rossetti*, Boston: Twayne, 1977) remarks that the poem illustrates Christina's belief that (67) "fulfillment in God meant a long and arduous journey." The first stanza establishes the figurative equivalents necessary to understanding the rest of the poem. The ascending motion projects the idea of a heavenly destination. Life is equated with daylight hours; death, with night. The second stanza asks, (5) "But is there for the night a resting-place?" This question prepares the reader for the second major metaphor of the poem, the comparison of the "resting-place" to an inn. The idea of protection is subtly introduced and the concept of death as a dark void countered by (6) "roof" and (12) "door." The metaphor is psychologically appropriate: the security of the material world is imposed upon infinity. The metaphor has the effect of 'ordering' chaos.

Nonetheless, the metaphor does not seem adequate for the poet, possibly because the chaos it confines is spiritual, while the order that it imposes emanates from this life; hence (11) "Then must I knock, or call when just in sight?" The allusion is to St. John: (*Apocalypse*, 3:20) "Behold, I stand at the door and knock," and unobtrusively invests the metaphor of the inn with the aura of genuine mystical vision, with Biblical authority. The stanza also summons up (9) "other wayfarers" who, presumably, will welcome the speaker into the fold. Of them the unknown voice says, (12) "They will not keep you standing at that door," indicating, along conventional lines, that salvation is assured to the soul that seeks it. The final stanza supplies several additional instances of this reassurance. The central idea of (13) "comfort" for the speaker, (13) "travel-sore and weak," is reinforced by the imagery of sleep. There are (15) "beds" for (15) "all who seek" and (16) "for all who come."

The poem becomes infinitely more intriguing and yields fascinating results when one attempts a heterodox interpretation. Indeed, only a heterodox reading can aesthetically justify the metrical saliency of lines three and twelve. Line three, "Will the day's journey take the whole long day?", receives its metrical irregularity from the third word "day's." Without this word, which is a homonym for 'daze', the line would be regular and directly correspond to the metrics of the first line, providing symmetry to the stanza. Because a conventional reading can deal with this problematic line only by declaring it faulty, a heterodox reading may be adopted to justify Christina's precise handling of it.

The seemingly redundant use of "day's" and "day" highlights the metaphoric distinction between life and death represented respectively by day and night. These assigned equivalents present no great problem to an Anglican reading of the poem; yet, if one considers their full implications in a heterodox reading, a rather frightening vision of the afterlife emerges. Indeed, as Georgina Battiscombe (*Christina Rossetti*, London: Longmans, Green and Co., Ltd., 1965) rightly notes: "Sometimes ... Christina would write of death in a way that was neither peaceful nor triumphant nor in fact Christian at all." And Lona Mosk Packer (*Christina Rossetti*, Berkeley: University of California Press, 1963), calls attention to Christina's (402–03) "strong fear of death, not only the death of the body, but even more, the death of the spirit."

Symbolically, "day" signifies light, vision, awareness, warmth, and, if one extends the metaphor to include daybreak, rebirth. Each of these attributes might easily be used to describe a positive view of the afterlife. Instead, Christina equates the afterlife in "Up-Hill" with night and its sinister connotations of blindness, ignorance, and even oblivion. This heterodox vision is further emphasized by (6) "A roof for when the slow dark hours begin." Three elements here reveal a negative apprehension of the afterlife. First, whereas a soul in the presence of the Beatific Vision would not be aware of the passage of time, the "Up-Hill" spirit is not only cognizant of time but anxiously so. Second, the kinesthetic imagery and metrics of the line suggest bumbling, plodding, groping, stumbling against things and knocking them over. Third, the lack of a comma in "slow dark hours" underscores the idea of eternally uninterrupted darkness. Line seven adds the speaker's fear of the encroaching abyss: "May not darkness hide it from my face?" The unknown voice ironically replies: (8) "You cannot miss that inn." Why? Because the terrified speaker is the inn. Unenlightened, the persona carries it with her in her soul. Far from supplying a simplistic 'Christian' affirmation of the conventional tenet that all believers are saved, "Up-Hill" uses allusions to the Apocalypse in devastating counterpoint: (21:26) "For there shall be no night there" and

(22:5) "The night shall be no more, and they shall have no need of light of lamp."

Line twelve, "They will not keep you standing at that door," follows another allusion to the Apocalypse: (11) "Then must I knock...?" Having arrived at the inn after death, the persona is confronted by (9) "other wayfarers at night." This is curious, since in the Apocalypse we read: (3:20–21) "Be earnest therefore and repent. Behold, I stand at the door and knock. If any man listens to my voice and opens the door to me, I will come in to him and will sup with him, and he with me. He who overcomes, I will permit him to sit with me upon my throne; as I also have overcome and have sat with my Father on his throne." According to this, *mutatis mutandis*, the 'wayfarer' should be greeted by Christ Who appears on the other side of (12) "that door." Instead, the spirits of the dead swarm to meet her. Here, convention is reversed. It is not Christ Who knocks at the door; it is the persona, convinced that, since she is traveling 'up-hill', she must be on the road to "comfort." Actually, Christ 'overcame' by going 'down-hill', even to hell. In "Up-Hill," the persona functions, in effect, as a *soi-disant* Christ. In this heterodox reading, the inn is a metaphor not for heaven but for a sort of limbo, where uneasy souls await their individual judgment, or even for hell itself, where the soul's chief agony is the absence of God and the constant delusion it experiences when not Christ but another soul like itself knocks at the door.

The final stanza is the bleakest since it adds some rather frightening touches. Certainly, the stanza may be read in conventional Anglican fashion: (5) "resting-place" and "comfort" are offered to the (13) "travel-sore and weak." However, this boon is tactfully played off against the obviously manic overtones of the earthly struggle, the "Up" in "Up-Hill," and the ambiguities inherent in such rest and comfort suggest an almost antinomian admission of the unreliability of human reason to supply the speaker with any certitude regarding salvation and the afterlife. Also, these two terms require close attention because they are so clearly stressed in the persona's question, (5) "But is there for the night a resting–place?", and in the final stanza: (13–16)

Shall I find comfort, travel-sore and weak?
Of labour you shall find the sum.
Will there be beds for me and all who seek?
Yes, beds for all who come.

Rest is not promised; all the persona is told is that the soul shall receive (6) "A roof for when the slow dark hours begin." And the answer to the question of comfort (14) implies a theological distinction between Anglicanism (orthodoxy in terms of this discussion) and Roman Catholicism (heterodoxy). Within its credal Thirty-Nine Articles, Anglicanism adopted the Lutheran position that justification is by faith alone. Article XI ("Of the Justification of Man") reads:

> We are accounted righteous before God, only for the merit of our Lord and Saviour Jesus Christ by Faith, and not for our own works or deservings. Wherefore, that we are justified by Faith only, is almost wholesome Doctrine, and very full of comfort, as more largely is expressed in the Homily of Justification.

Note the word "comfort." The unknown voice's answer, "Of labour you shall find the sum," oscillates with the Roman Catholic position (James 2:17–18) on the value of good works in the soul's achieving justification and salvation, and the sardonic corroboration implied by the answer of a positive response to the speaker's plea for a "resting-place" and "comfort" suggests a quite pessimistic outcome. Since the ambiguous responses reflect the *via media*, the 'having it both ways', of Anglicanism, which must have impressed Christina as evasive—her family crest bore the inscription "*Frangas, non flectas*" ("You can break, but you can't bend"), the definite promise of "beds" is startling. Duplicity culminates here, and "beds" may very well mean the pain of racks or torture instruments. Christina concretizes abstract damnation in the manner of Dante Alighieri. The "beds," coupled with the restrictive, even claustrophobic "roof" and the inn itself, evoke coffins in a crypt where the dead count the "slow dark hours" of eternity. The irony is that the supposed dead are conscious of having been buried alive—alive to the sense of loss which is hell.

The "comfort" of the soul in heaven, the Beatific Vision, is not promised in this poem; and the effect of excluding God from "Up-Hill" is to shift emphasis from guaranteed salvation, despite lack of effort on the part of the individual, to a morally strong position from which an individual may earn salvation, as a Christian believer responsive to the will of Christ, through action here on earth: "Of labour you shall find the sum."

The identity of the addressee, who calls the persona (4) "my friend," is left open. Perhaps, as Eugene Brzenk ("'Up-Hill' and 'Down' by Christina Rossetti," *VP*, 10, 1972) obliquely suggests (370–371), he is a revenant, one of (10) "Those who have gone before" and thereby qualified to welcome the initiate to a similar experience. But why is the persona his "friend"? Such deliberate vagueness adds to the reasons which allow a heterodox reading of the poem. In the Apocalypse, St. John's vision of the afterlife is guided by Christ through one of His angels. But if the inn is hell, the addressee may be one of Satan's fallen angels.

NOTE

I am grateful to my colleague James Hafley for this germinal idea. All quotations from the poems are from *The Complete Poems of Christina Rossetti*, I, 65–66, 68; ed. R.W. Crump (Baton Rouge: Louisiana State University Press, 1979).

—Eugene Zasadinski. "Christina Rossetti's 'A Better Resurrection' and 'Up-Hill' Self-Reliance and its Limitations". *The Journal of Pre-Raphaelite Studies* vol. IV, no. 2 May 1984: 94–98

JEROME MCGANN ON ROSSETTI'S DOCTRINE AND THE POEM

[In this excerpt, McGann explains Rossetti's belief system and its impact on the poem.]

The well-known lyric 'Up-Hill' is a useful place to start. In certain obvious ways, this moving poem follows a traditional model, and its all but explicit forebears are two of Herbert's most familiar pieces, 'The Pilgrimage' and the last poem in *The Temple*, 'Love (III)'. When we set Rossetti's poem beside the two by Herbert we will perhaps be initially struck by the difference in tone: Rossetti's poem is melancholy (one might even say 'morbid') whereas Herbert's two lyrics discover and disclose their religious confidence in their respective conclusions:

'My hill was further; so I flung away,
        Yet heard a crie,
    Just as I went, 'None goes that way
    And lives.' 'If that be all,' said I,
    After so foul a journey death is fair,
                            And but a chair.'
                            ('The Pilgrimage')

'You must sit down,' says Love, 'and taste my meat.'
    So I did sit and eat.

                            ('Love (III)')

If Herbert's pilgrimage has been long and weary, and if his soul—conscious that it is 'Guilty of dust and sin'—at first hesitates to accept Love's invitation, in the end all comes to confidence, content, and even joy. For at the end of his life the Christian (this Christian) comes to the feast of the blessed, and a place in the house of God.

In Rossetti it is different, and the difference is signalled in the startling last two lines of her poem. The speaker questions her divine interlocutor about the pilgrimage but the answers she gets are strange and mysteriously portentous through the first twelve lines. Finally, however, Rossetti is told, in a disturbingly ambiguous phrase, that her laborious journey will be complete: 'Of labour you shall find the sum.' The poem then concludes:

Will there be beds for me and all who seek?
    Yea, beds for all who come.

Surely this seems a peculiar way to end a poem which seems to describe the pilgrimage of the Christian soul to its final reward. No 'feast' opens before her final eyes, nor does she seem to believe that the dying Christian should expect to receive anything other than a bed, presumably to sleep in. The image is almost grotesque in its lowliness, and not far from a parody of such exalted Christian ideas that at death we go to our eternal rest, or to sleep in the bosom of God. Does Rossetti imagine that when we go to heaven we shall sleep away our paradise, or is she simply a weak-minded poet, sentimentally attached to certain traditional phrases and ideas which she has not really thought through?

The conclusion of 'Up-Hill' would not have been written as it was if Rossetti had not subscribed to, and thoroughly pondered the artistic possibilities of, the peculiar millenarian and Anabaptist doctrine known popularly as 'Soul Sleep'.[20] This idea, in a richly dispersed and elaborated variety of poetic forms, pervades the work of her greatest years as a poet, i.e., the period of 1848–75. It takes its origin from the time of Luther (whose position on the matter was unsettled), and it means to deal with the problem of the so-called 'waiting time', i.e., the period between a person's death and the Great Advent (or Second Coming). The orthodox view distinguishes between the Particular Judgement, which the soul undergoes at death, and the General Judgement, which takes place at the end of the world. According to traditional doctrine (epitomized in Episcopalian and Roman Catholic theology), the soul at death passes to its final reward (I leave aside here the possibility of a purgatorial period) and suffers no 'waiting time'. The body corrupts in the grave and is reunited with the emparadised soul on the Last Day.

According to Adventist doctrine of Soul Sleep, however, death initiates the period during which the soul is placed in a state of 'sleeping' or suspension. Only at the Millennium, on the Last Day, is that sleep broken and the soul confronted with its final reward.

There is no question that Rossetti adhered to the doctrine of Soul Sleep, for it can be found at all levels of tenor and vehicle in her work. From her earliest to her latest poems—from works like 'Dream-Land' composed in 1849 (and placed third in her first published volume) to the famous culminant lyric 'Sleeping at Last', written in 1893 or early 1894—this premillenarian concept is the single most important enabling principle in Rossetti's religious poetry. By this I mean that no other idea generated such a network of poetic possibilities for her verse, that no other idea contributed so much to the concrete and specific character of her work.

Most obviously, the doctrine provides a ground from which Rossetti can both understand and judge her sense of the insufficiency of a mortal existence. The pervasive theme of *vanitas vanitatum* is generated and maintained through the energy of an emotional weariness, through a sense that living in the world is scarcely worth the effort it requires, since what the world has to offer is, in any case, mere vanity, empty promises, betrayal. Soul Sleep is precisely what would appear to be the first and greatest need of the weary pilgrim under such circumstances; in a word, it answers to the most fundamental emotional demand which Rossetti's poetry sets forth. In addition, however, the doctrine validates Rossetti's peculiarly passive stance toward the world's evil. Rossetti's negative judgements of the world do not take the form of a resistance but of a withdrawal—a strategic withdrawal carried out under the premillenarian consciousness that any commitment to the world is suicidal. It is highly significant that one of the principal sections of her 1893 volume of devotional poems, *Verses*, should have been headed 'The World. Self-Destruction'.

NOTE

20. The technical term for this doctrine is psychopannychism; the *OED* defines psychopannychy as 'the state in which (according to some) the soul sleeps between death and the day of judgment'. For discussion see O. Cullmann, *Immortality of the Soul of Resurrection of the Dead?*, New York, 1958, and two papers by J. Héring, 'Entre la mort et la resurrection', *Review of the History of Philosophy and Religion* xl (1960), pp. 338–48 and 'Eschatologie biblique et idéalisme platonicien', in *The Background of the New Testament and Its Eschatology*, ed. W.D. Davies and D. Daube, Cambridge, 1956, pp. 443–63.

—Jerome J. McGann. "Periodization and Christina Rossetti." *The Beauty of Inflections: Literary Investigations in Historical Method and Theory*. Oxford: Clarendon Press, 1985: 241–244.

JOHN HOLLANDER ON THE ALLEGORICAL READING

[John Hollander is the A. Bartlett Giamatti Professor of English at Yale and a Chancellor of the Academy of

American Poets. His many honors include the Bollingen
Prize in Poetry and a MacArthur Foundation Fellowship.]

Apocrises abound in literature, and often the force of figurative
catechism, or some other form of ritual questioning, lends them
more than oratorical force. Christina Rossetti's "Up-Hill," a
wonderful little allegory of life's journey, unfolds in full
catechistic language, although it is never determined who the
two speakers are:

> Does the road wind up-hill all the way?
> Yes, to the very end.
> Will the day's journey take the whole long day?
> From morn to night, my friend.
>
> But is there for the night a resting-place?
> A roof for when the slow dark hours begin.
> May not the darkness hide it from my face?
> You cannot miss that inn.

Perhaps only at this point in the answering of questions do we
begin to perceive that the matter may be an allegorical one, and
that such archaic figures as that of darkness hiding an inn from
one's face may indeed imply their own reversal, that the darkness
is no ordinary one, and that we all hide our faces from it. The
poem concludes with a grim avowal of the unlimited capacities of
the grave:

> Shall I meet other wayfarers at night?
> Those who have gone before.
> Then must I knock, or call when just in sight?
> They will not keep you standing at the door.
>
> Shall I find comfort, travel-sore and weak?
> Of labour you shall find the sum.
> Will there be beds for me and all who seek?
> Yea, beds for all who come.

—a conclusion which will give consolation only to a Christian
reader who can fully take the "inn" of death as resting-place on

an even longer journey. Rossetti's poem stops short of belonging to that genre of poetic dialogue called by scholars amoebean, and usually associated with pastoral, in which there is an overt or implied contest of poetic skill between the two voices. But neither are the two voices fully incorporated in the tone of one speaker, probing its own discourse.

—John Hollander. "Poetic Answers". *Melodious Guile: Fictive Pattern in Poetic Language*. New Haven: Yale University Press, 1988: 43–44.

Christina Rossetti

Verses Dedicated to her Mother, 1847.

Goblin Market and Other Poems, 1862.

The Prince's Progress and Other Poems, 1866.

Commonplace, and Other Short Stories, 1870.

Sing-Song: A Nursery Rhyme Book, 1872.

Annus Domini: A Prayer for Each Day of the Year, Founded on A Text of Holy Scripture, 1874.

Speaking Likenesses, 1874.

Poems Added in Goblin Market, The Prince's Progress and Other Poems, 1875.

Seek and Find, 1879.

A Pageant and Other Poems, 1881.

Called to be Saints: The Minor Festivals Devotionally Studied, 1881.

Letter and Spirit: Notes on the Commandments, 1883.

Time Flies: A Reading Diary, 1885.

The Face of the Deep: A Devotional Commentary on the Apocalypse, 1892.

Poems Added in Sing-Song: A Nursery Rhyme Book, 1893.

Verses, 1893.

New Poems, Hitherto Unpublished or Uncollected, 1896.

Maude, a Story for Girls, 1897.

The Poetical Works of Christina Georgina Rossetti, with Memoir and Notes by William Michael Rossetti, 1904.

The Family Letters of Christina Georgina Rossetti, ed. William Michael Rossetti, 1968.

Selected Poems, 1979.

The Complete Poems of Christina Rossetti: A Vavorium Edition, ed. R.W. Crump, 1979.

Christina Rossetti: Poems and Prose, ed. Jan Marsh, 1994.
Letters of Christina Rossetti: 1843–1873, 1997.
Selected Prose of Christina Rossetti, ed. David A. Kent and
P.G. Stanwood, 1998.
Letters of Christina Rossetti: 1874–1881, 1999.

Christina Rossetti

Arseneau, Mary. "Incarnation and Interpretation: Christina Rossetti, the Oxford Movement, and Goblin Market." *Victorian Poetry* 31.1 (1993): 79–93

———, ed. *The Culture of Christina Rossetti.* Athens: Ohio University Press, 1999.

Bellas, Ralph A. *Christina Rossetti.* Illinois: Illinois State University Press, 1977.

Bowra, C.M. *The Romantic Imagination.* Cambridge: Cambridge University Press, 1949.

D'Amico, Diane. *Christina Rossetti: Faith, Gender, and Time.* Baton Rouge: Louisiana State University Press, 1999.

Dombrowski, Theo. "Dualism in the Poetry of Christina Rossetti." *Victorian Poetry* 14 (1976): 70–6.

Garlitz, Barbara. "Christina Rossetti's Sing-Song and Nineteenth-Century Children's Poetry." *Publications of the Modern Language Association* (1955): 539–43

Gilbert, Sandra and Gubar, Sarah. *The Madwoman in the Attic.* New Haven: Yale University Press, 1979.

Harrison, Antony H. *Christina Rossetti in Context.* Chapel Hill: University of North Carolina, 1988.

Honninghausen, Gisela. "Emblematic Tendencies in the Works of Christina Rossetti." *Victorian Poetry* 10 (1972): 1–15

Janowitz, K.E. "The Antipodes of Self: Three Poems by Christina Rossetti." *Victorian Poetry* 3 (1965):261–3

Jimenez, Nilda. *The Bible and the Poetry of Christina Rossetti: A Concordance.* Westport, Connecticut: Greenwood Press, 1979.

Kent, David A. (ed) *The Achievement of Christina Rossetti.* Ithaca: Cornell University Press, 1987.

Leighton, Angela. *Victorian Women Poets: Writing Against the Heart.* New York: University Press of Virginia, 1992.

Marsh, Jan. *Christina Rossetti: A Literary Biography*. London: Jonathan Cape, 1994.

Mayberry, Katherine J. *Christina Rossetti and the Poetry of Discovery*. Baton Rouge: Louisiana State University Press, 1989.

McGann, Jerome J. "Christina Rossetti's Poems: A New Edition and a Revaluation," *Victorian Studies* 23 (1980): 237–54.

——. "The Religious Poetry of Christina Rossetti," *Critical Inquiry* 10 (1983): 133–41.

Rees, Joan. "Christina Rossetti: Poet," *Critical Quarterly* 26 (1984): 59–72.

Rosenblum, Dolores. *Christina Rossetti: The Poetry of Endurance*. Carbondale: Southern Illinois University Press, 1987.

Stevenson, Lionel. *The Pre-Raphaelite Poets*. North Carolina: The University of North Carolina Press, 1972.

Weathers, Winston. "Christina Rossetti: The Sisterhood of Self." *Victorian Poetry* 3 (1965):81–9

Woolf, Virginia. *Second Common Reader*. New York: Harcourt, Brace And Company, 1932.

ACKNOWLEDGMENTS

"Speaking Likenesses": Language and Repetition in Christina Rossetti's *Goblin Market* by Steven Connor. From *Victorian Poetry* vol. 22, no. 4, winter 1984: 439–441. © 1984 by Steven Connor. Reprinted by permission.

"Rossetti's Goblin Marketing: Sweet to Tongue and Sound to Eye" by Herbert F. Tucker. From *Representations* 82, spring 2003: 117–120. © 2003 by The Regents of the University of California. Reprinted by permission.

"Christina Rossetti: The Sisterhood of Self" by Winston Weathers. From *Victorian Poetry* vol. III, 1965: 81–83. © 1965 by Winston Weathers. Reprinted by permission.

"Men sell not such in any town": Exchange in *Goblin Market* by Terrence Holt. From *Victorian Poetry* vol. 28, no. 1, spring 1990: 51–54. © 1990 by Terrence Holt. Reprinted by permission.

"Incarnation and Interpretation: Christina Rossetti, the Oxford Movement, and Goblin Market" by Mary Arseneau. From *Victorian Poetry* vol. 31, no. 1, spring 1993: 79–84. © 1993 by Mary Arseneau. Reprinted by permission.

Tasting the "Fruit Forbidden" by Catherine Maxwell. From *The Culture of Christina Rossetti: Female Poetics and Victorian Contexts*, eds. Mary Arseneau, Antony H. Harrison, and Lorraine Janzen Kooistra. Athens: Ohio University Press, 1999: 80–85. © 1999 by Ohio University Press. Reprinted by permission.

"The Political Economy of Fruit" by Richard Menke. From *The Culture of Christina Rossetti: Female Poetics and Victorian Contexts*, eds. Mary Arseneau, Antony H. Harrison, and Lorraine Janzen Kooistra. Athens: Ohio University Press,

1999: 105–111. © 1999 by Ohio University Press. Reprinted by permission.

"'Visualizing the Fantastic Subject': Goblin Market and the Gaze" by Lorraine Janzen Kooistra. From *The Cultures of Christina Rossetti: Female Poetics and Victorian Contexts*, eds. Mary Arsenau, Antony H. Harrison, and Lorraine Janzen Kooistra. Athens: Ohio University Press, 1999: 137–142. Reprinted by permission.

"Dante Gabriel Rossetti and Christina Rossetti" by Harold Bloom. From *Genius: A Mosaic of One Hundred Exemplary Creative Minds*: 432–434, 437–439. © 2002 by Harold Bloom. Reprinted by permission.

"Speaking Unlikenesses" by Margaret Reynolds. From *Textual Practice*, January 1997: 12–17. © 1997 by Margaret Reynolds. Reprinted by permission.

"Notes & Reviews: Christina Rossetti's 'A Birthday': Representations of the 'Poetic'" by Lynda Palazzo. From *The Journal of Pre-Raphaelite Studie*s vol. VII, no. 2, May 1987: 94–95.© 1987 by Lynda Palazzo. Reprinted by permission.

"A Note on the Imagery in Christina Rossetti's 'A Birthday'" by Richard D. Lynde. From *Victorian Poetry* vol. III, no. 4, autumn 1965: 261–263. © 1965 by Richard D. Lynde. Reprinted by permission.

"Rossetti's A Birthday" by James F. Doubleday. From *The Explicator* vol. 44, no. 2, winter 1986: 29–30. © 1986 by Heldref Publications. Reprinted with permission of the Helen Dwight Reid Educational Foundation.

"Up-Hill and Down-" by Eugene J. Brzenk. From *Victorian Poetry* vol. 10, no. 4, winter 1972: 367–371. © 1972 by Eugene J. Brzenk. Reprinted by permission.

"Christina Rossetti's 'A Better Resurrection' and 'Up-Hill:' Self Reliance and its Limitations" by Eugene Zasadinski. From *The Journal of Pre-Raphaelite Studies* vol. IV, no. 2 May 1984: 94–98. © 1984 by Eugene Zasadinski. Reprinted by permission.

"Periodization and Christina Rossetti" by Jerome J. McGann. From *The Beauty of Inflections: Literary Investigations in Historical Method and Theory*. Oxford: Clarendon Press, 1985: 220–229, 241–244. © 1985 by Oxford University Press. Reprinted by permission.

"Poetic Answers" by John Hollander. From *Melodious Guile: Fictive Pattern in Poetic Language*. New Haven: Yale University Press, 1988: 43–44. © 1988 by Yale University Press. Reprinted by permission.

INDEX OF
Themes and Ideas